MY ISSUES TOUCH
THE HEART OF GOD

By Rev. Carolyn Baker

Order this book online at www.trafford.com
or email orders@trafford.com

Most Trafford titles are also available at major online book retailers.

Printed in United States of America.

ISBN: 978-1-4269-2978-6 (sc)
ISBN: 978-1-4269-2980-9 (e)

Library of Congress Control Number: 2010904065

Trafford rev. 11/15/2013

 www.trafford.com

North America & international
toll-free: 1 888 232 4444 (USA & Canada)
fax: 812 355 4082

Acknowledgments

I would like to acknowledge my husband of twenty years, Christopher Dean Baker. Thank you for your love and patience.

I give thanks to my daughter, Angel E. Coleman, for her encouragement and support during the times I wanted to give up and for her smile of approval when I felt too tired to go on.

I wish to thank Deborah Lynn Kearse for her commitment and the time she spent editing this book. Your dedication to this work is well appreciated.

And finally, I want to thank Dr. Ernestine Roberts for pushing me and encouraging me to write this book.

Foreword

It is remarkable that God uses people to transmit experience to alleviate their pain and suffering.

What Carolyn endured goes beyond the pale. From conception to formal training this young lady will take you from grief to grace and from shame to gain.

You will no longer look at your trial as a tragedy but ferment to heal the hurting and a camera to look into human experience at its worst and to see God's hand at work to turn what was horrible into something wonderful.

Carolyn now lives a fulfilling life helping others to take the limits off and see their issues touching God and touching others.

Read this work with your heart and see how much value it provides for those who want to breathe and truly live

This is not for the faint of heart but for those who desire to regain their strength.

Here it is real and authentic. Open your eyes and open your heart and began to see that life is not a rose without thorns but with them is a fragrance that inspired you to buy another.

Read "My Issues Touch the Heart of God" and allow it to touch your heart and see your life become better.

Archbishop LeRoy Bailey, Jr.
Senior Pastor of the First Cathedral

Dedication

This book is dedicated to my three daughters who unknowingly gave me a reason to hope and strive for a better life. To my sister, Revon (aka "Patsy"), for always having my back, though often times it meant she would be alone. Again, I say thank you. To my Pastor, Archbishop LeRoy Bailey, Jr. of the First Cathedral in Bloomfield, CT, and First Lady, Rev. Mother Reathie Bailey, for their love and support. The lessons I've learned under their tutelage have taken me to a plateau I've never before experienced. To Apostle Ardean Richardson, pastor of Holy Ghost Deliverance Cathedral in Bridgeport, CT, for her loving kindness, her beautiful smile that warms any heart, and, of course, her prayers. Her friendship is irreplaceable.

"Just then a woman who had been subject to bleeding for twelve years came up behind him and touched the edge of his cloak. She said to herself, "If I only touch his cloak, I will be healed." Jesus turned and saw her. "Take heart, daughter," he said, "your faith has healed you." And the woman was healed from that moment." (Matthew 9:20-22 - NIV)

****

Many may say that this book is long over due. At this time I still am not sure what God wanted me to do but to keep the faith, keep other people's mouths off of me for not doing what He wanted me to do, and to share my life story with the world. I am writing this book in the hopes that God will use it to change someone's life. I guess the very beginning would be the best place to start, but let me assure you I can only go back as far as God will allow my mind to go.

I birthed the demon of abandonment and rejection as a fetus in my mother's womb. My mother was five months pregnant with me when I heard my father tell her, "I know you got another young one (meaning baby or child) in there, but I told you I did not want any kids. I let you have the first one, but this one I do not want any parts of." Yes, I heard this when I was in my mother's womb. After he said this, he walked off. My mother was washing clothes from a big black wash pot in the back yard. The Spirit allowed me to see all of this so I could understand that what was going on was really true. I then saw my mother putting her hands between her legs, falling to her knees and beginning to cry very hard. When I was born I had a birth mark of two hands between my thighs. I never knew where they came from until after I got saved and God gave me this vision. I believe God gave me this vision to deliver me from disliking my mother so much and blaming her for everything wrong in my life, while giving my father all the love and positive feedback.

That was the beginning of my issues. When I was four years old my mother left North Carolina and moved to Connecticut. She left me and my brother with my dad's sister and her husband and children. They are a very close and loving family, as I have always known them to be. We lived on a farm with my uncle and aunt, and the smell of fresh air and the sweet smell of food cooking was always in my nose. Going to live with them was ok until my mother stopped sending money to them. I had never heard or seen these two people fussing or having any disagreement until one night when we got home late from a church function at the Virginia state fair. I was lying in bed, and I guess they thought all of us where asleep after the long day we just had, but I heard them speaking in a harsh tone to one another about me and my brother. My brother is my heart I love him today like he is my own son. We went through so much together as kids on into our adulthood. However, this story is about me. My aunt was fussing with my uncle about my mother not sending money to them in about six months. She said they could not keep us and buy clothes for us. She said, "Feeding them is no problem, but that boy and that gal are growing. How does she expect us to clothe her kids? We have our own in the backroom. I told her we could give them a good, loving home, a roof over their heads, along with our own, and put food in their mouths, but she had to send money down here to help out. I'll give them to their daddy if she thinks I won't let her not send some money down here before that boy starts to go to school." My dad was a chronic alcoholic. This is why my mother did not want us with him. Anyway, my uncle, God bless him, said these words: "No, we are not going to put the children out nor give them to your brother. She asked us to keep her children, and we're just going to have to do what we can to make it. And we can make it. You and I have been down this way before when we first started with our family. Let's just give her some time. Maybe hard times have laid on her up there. We don't know. She has not written us and told us anything yet." My uncle loves me and my brother as his own children until this day. I love him and thank God for both him and my aunt. He is now battling cancer, but God has kept him thus far. Glory to God! I just praise Him for this man's heart of love. Church was always in me, I guess you could say. I just never had the opportunity at that stage in my life for anything to mature.

Let's get back to the seed planter in my life: my "dad". You see, the Bible says there is power in the tongue so we need to watch over words that we speak. I just want to show how the words spoken out of my father's mouth could be bad seeds. My dad rejected me and abandoned me by the words he spoke to my mom while I was in her womb.

Children, even before they are born, can hear words as well as music as they are developing in the womb. So be very careful what you put out in the atmosphere for your unborn child to hear. Be careful where you take that unborn child as well as what you feed them. My mother and father fed me alcohol quite often, as I will discuss later.

At some point while I was living with my aunt and uncle, my dad started coming around on weekends. I can only guess that my aunt had sent for him. I had a child's love for him but I did not really know him. I was only about four or five years old and had not seen him before that time. So I was glad to see him but he was not my uncle, did not smell like my uncle. However, my uncle would not let me or my brother call him "daddy" like the kids did around the house. When I ask him why not and told him that I loved him, he smiled and said "I know you do baby girl, but I'm not your real father. I'm your uncle and I love you too, but if you call me 'daddy' what will your real daddy think?" I said, "I don't care; I do not know him any way." I then asked if I could call him "uncle dad." He picked me up, gave me a big hug and said, "Oh, baby girl, uncle would like that." He became my dad from that moment on. The only other man that I have looked at as a father is my pastor, Archbishop LeRoy Bailey, Jr. I love him more than I can express. I know God has shown him my love for him. He has watched over my life to help bring about the changes that have taken place in me. God has healed and filled so many holes in my life through him.

But back to my father. My aunt did all the girls' hair on Saturday morning so she wouldn't have to do it on Sunday morning before church service. There were six girls including me. She always did my hair last because she said my hair was not as thick as the other girls'. My aunt and uncle never did anything for their kids that they didn't do for us, as well. I need to share that now because later on you will see how things changed for me. It was on one of these Saturdays that my dad came over drunk as a skunk. I knew what that smell was that made him stink to me: it was alcohol. He stayed until we had lunch and then the adults got together to talk while I went outside to play with my youngest cousin. All of a sudden, I heard my dad begin to yell and curse really loud. I ran to the house and stepped through the door just in time to see my uncle grab his rifle from over the door and tell my father to get off his property and never ever come back. He said, "You are no longer welcome here. You will not come into our home and talk to my wife the way you are speaking to her. I don't do it and you won't either." I saw him point the gun at my father and at the same time my aunt and I both said, "No!!!" I screamed, "Don't hurt anybody, uncle! Please don't!" I was scared out of my little mind because I had never seen my uncle upset. He was always a pleasant-spirited man; always soft spoken and quiet. My uncle did not appear to have a mean or rough bone in his body. He cared for everybody, so my dad had to have said something really bad to get my uncle keyed up like that. After my uncle saw me, he put the gun to his side. I could tell he was still heated, but he pointed to the door and said, "It's best you leave now. You have upset this family for the last time. My dad walked off, but not before saying, "I'll be back for my kids. You just wait."

After dinner in the front room, my uncle told us he was sorry that we had to see him act that way. We told him it was ok, but I only said it because his kids said it. I still did not know what was this craziness was all about. My mind said I was too young to know these things, so just as I was about to relax in my mind he called me to him. His eyes did not look right. I sat on his lap, which was like a holiday treat because we only sat on his lap during holidays. Anyway, he sat me on his lap and spoke these words while looking at my brother: "Boy, this is your only sister." Then he looked at me and said, "He is your only brother that we know of. I need you two to always take care of each other no matter where you are. Look out for one another. Can you remember to do that for me?" Still not fully understanding what was going on, my brother and I both said, "Yes." I was listening then because I had another seed planted in me by my uncle and that was to take care of my brother no matter what. I had to listen, learn and know what was going on. From that day on I had a need to watch over my brother, to protect him.

Later on my aunt was in the kitchen and this short lady came in who was said to be my grandmother. She had moved closer to town but was coming back to the family's smaller house up the road. She looked at me and said, "She sure looks just like her daddy, just like that man." My aunt asked her who did she think I would look like. It seemed like I was always around adults because I was a girl and had to stay around the house with my aunt and little cousin. We were both girls so we both were always with my aunt. My aunt told my grandmother that my father was supposed to have brought money by for us, but that he had come over drunk that Saturday and did not have the money. She told my grandmother that he started getting nasty with her in front of my uncle just because he was her brother, but that my uncle was not going to stand for that nonsense in his house and she was going to stick by her husband no matter what anybody said. My aunt repeated what my father said about taking me and my brother from them and told my grandmother that my uncle looked him right in the face and told my dad that he was not going to get us because my mother made my uncle promise that he would keep me and my brother. My aunt thought my dad was getting worse with his drinking. He was fighting people all over town and the word was getting out about him. My aunt was very close to my dad and I could tell she was hurt behind his behavior.

Well, summer began to heat up. There were always picnics and cookouts. It was a great summer until my dad showed up. That's when things got crazy again and my life was gone for good. Then the day came when my uncle, with tears in his eyes, told me and my brother that our father was moving us to live with him. I looked at my uncle and said, "But we don't want to go. We want to stay with you." He hugged us and said that my dad would bring us over to visit. It was settled. We had to go with my dad and there was nothing my uncle could do. He tried to make us feel better by telling us that our dad was going to be really good to us, just like he was. My brother just stood there like the life had been sucked completely out of him. He did not say a word. My uncle then reminded us about what he had asked us to do: take care of each other no matter what. We shook our head between the tears and were then carried off to hell. My father took us to his house somewhere. I was crying so hard that I did not remember which way he had turned. I did not know which way to run. We were stuck.

It was the Fourth of July. All the boys and men were playing with firecrackers. The girls could not play with them. My father gave one to my brother on that porch of his house, but my brother did not want to hold one. My father had men friends with him and one woman who I later learned was his drunken girlfriend. My brother did not want to throw the firecracker, but my father lit it anyway and tried to give it to him. My brother refused and it blew up in his hand. My dad was embarrassed by my brother and slapped him upside the head. Well, it was on then. I remembered what my uncle said and I charged my little behind into my father, hitting and kicking him. He grabbed and shook me. The men said, "Don't you hit that child, man." My father then said these words: "I'll tear her little tail up. She's just like that mama of hers."

My father left that day after he was told by his friend not to hit me. He left with these people and told me and my brother that he would be back and to go in the house before it got dark. I cannot say if he came back that night but I do know he was back and forth for about two weeks. I do not remember my father ever coming back to that house. After the summer months it began to get dark earlier and earlier. My brother and I were left out there on that farm alone. We had little food and then we had no food. As it got colder we had no matches or wood left to make a fire. My brother and I drank sugar water and I believe we ate flour because we had no food. I'm sharing this to show that God, even when we do not know Him, will keep and protect and provide for us. At night my brother and I would huddle up together in the big bed to keep warm. I would urinate in the bed because I was afraid to go outside in the dark. This went on for months.

No one ever came down the road to see about us. My dad had not come home in months. We were left on a farm - a four year old and a six years old. We kept looking out the window at night and playing in the front yard during the day. It never crossed our minds to leave and start walking down that road. My father had told us not to leave the yard and that was it. One night we went to bed and I asked my brother if he thought dad was coming for us that night. He said, "I don't know. Just go to sleep." I was so cold. My brother told me to lay closer to him to keep warm. Then I started to cry. I wanted to go "home", back to my uncle's house. My brother said he did not know how to get there without getting lost. He again told me to go to sleep. I lay down and cried myself to sleep. All of a sudden, I heard a car outside. I thought it was our dad, but my brother told me to be quiet because it could have been a stranger. At that point I didn't care. Even though it was cold in the room, I jumped out of that bed and looked through the curtains. I saw a fair-skinned man in a white shirt. My brother told me to get back and be quiet before he hurt us. I was torn between listening to my brother because of what our uncle had told us and getting out of that cold place. I did not listen to my brother. I tried but something inside me prompted me to speak to the man. The man knocked on the door and I peeked out. He said he was lost and wanted to speak to my father or mother. I blurted out that they were not in the house. He then asked if there was an adult in the house who could give him directions. I told him we were there by ourselves. That's when the man became concerned and asked when our parents would be back. I told him I didn't know and that we had been there by ourselves for a long time but I didn't know how long. He asked if he could come inside, but we told him we couldn't open the door to strangers. The man told us we were doing the right thing and again asked us if we knew when our parents would be back. We told him no. He looked very sad and I guess he realized that we had been left alone for good.

The man indicated that he had a son and daughter about the age of me and my brother, and he went to his car to get them. Out stepped a young boy wearing a white shirt and a little girl about my height. They had fruit in their hands for me and my brother, but my brother still did not want to open the door. However, when I saw that food I pushed my brother out of the way and opened the door. The man handed us an apple, orange, and candy cane. He then asked us about other family members. We told him we only knew the names of our uncle and aunt but did not know where they lived. We only knew they had a really big farm. The man did not step into the house. He just looked around and asked if we would like to come with him to find our family. My brother was scared and he jumped back, pushing me at the same time, and closed the door. He said, "No, we have to stay here." The man stood outside the door and said, "Son, I'm going to go get some help for the two of you. I'll be back, OK?" Peace came over me and I told my brother that we would be leaving that place, never to return. My brother was more negative, not believing the man could find anybody that knew us.

You will not believe what happened next. That man found our mother at a club. He went into a club and was asking about a family with the last name of my uncle and aunt. My mom had just come into town that day and was at that club. Someone in the club turned down the jukebox so that the man could be heard asking about some kids that were left in a house alone. My mother overheard him and knew he was talking about us. She could not believe that my uncle had given us to that drunken father of ours. She finally came to the house looking and smelling so good. She was so pretty. Believe it or not, my dad came in just as she started to raise all kinds of hell. She saw him pull out a razor and he cut her hands. My mother took a swing at him, but he jumped back and ran away. Boy, that man flew. Now I felt safe from him.

Unfortunately, my mother did not stay pretty too long. She took us to her crazy sister's house who let her husband abuse her right in front of her kids. This aunt and uncle fought all the time. I remember one time her husband cut her ear one night with an ice pick. Boy, did that scare me. I stayed so close to my brother while living there that he never could play. He kept his eyes and ears open for me.

My mother's sister did not care for my dad's people so I do not know why she brought us to them instead of back to my "uncle dad's" house where we were loved. I remember on the days my brother went to school I would hide under the bed until he came home from school. He would give me his lunch and tell me not to let them see it. My mother's sister would feed us only after she fed her kids, and she hit me all the time. My brother could no longer handle the beating and the fighting that went on. Just like me, he was afraid to sleep at night. He did not want to leave me there in the daytime while he went to school but he had no other choice. One day he told me that we were going to run away and go back to my "uncle dad's" house. The school bus he rode on stopped at a market place that looked like the market my uncle used to take his son and my brother to with him. Our first plan did not work because my brother had too much yard work to do. However, a week later our plan fell into action. We were off to our aunt and uncle's house.

I was so glad as we walked the highway, not knowing that we had almost sixty miles to walk. We kept walking and walking. We had walked almost thirty miles when an old white man stopped and gave us a ride. He took us to a gas station and called my mother's sister. We were taken back got a bad beating. I told my brother the next time we don't take no ride from anybody; we just keep walking. My brother said that he did not want another beating like the one he had just gotten. "Lets just stay here," he said, "and you stay out of her way. She will not hit you so much." We talked some more and eventually my brother said, "Let's just wait before we try it again." I agreed, not knowing at the time that my aunt and uncle were at the filling station and had heard about two kids who had run away to find their "uncle dad." They knew it was me and my brother and asked where we had been taken.

I was in the house on Saturday afternoon and I saw this big, black, old, shiny car just like the one my uncle and aunt drove. I looked and froze because I knew if this was them we would be going home for good. When that quiet, loving man stepped out of that car and my tall aunt with her firm voice stepped out on the passenger side I thought I had died and gone to heaven. They came on the porch because that mean aunt of mine told me I had better not leave the porch. But when my uncle got near, I leaped on him and just kept asking him to let me go back with him. "He said, "Baby girl, I have to speak to your aunt here about that. I cannot just take you like that." She agreed to let us go back. She said, "Take all your stuff because you aren't ever coming back under my roof. I told your mother I did not want to do this any way, so get! These are your people now. Go with them." Boy, I was so glad. I did not have much to pack. It all would fit in a brown paper bag. No wonder I lived out of bags half my life.

I will never forget that Saturday as long as I live. We were packed and ready to leave, and my uncle, being the graceful man that he is, said to thank and hug our aunt - my mother's sister - for her help. I did not want to do anything but get my little, narrow behind in that big, black car and ride until I was sure I would never see those people ever again. We did as we were told, but I let her know I did not want to hug her. Again, I heard, "She is just like her mama." I never gave those words any thought at that age. Once again, we were off with the family that loved us. I believe we stayed there until I was six years old, just about time for me to start school. The day came when we were told that our mother was coming to get us to take us north with her along with my other brothers and sisters. I know there was something going on with the others. Remember, I said earlier I had more than just my brother that lived with me. We were together because we had the same daddy. I was taken to live with my mother's older sister who was the twin to the other nut that kept me and my brother before (the one we ran away from). This woman was married and had a pretty big family of her own. Her older kids tended to run the house, but she saw to everything the girls did. She ran her house like my "uncle dad" did, except there just wasn't a love connection there. Everything was done like a duty or chore and that's it. However, this aunt was not mean-spirited. There were so many kids there it was like a summer camp. Her older daughters had kids and their kids played with the mother's kids. It was strange.

We stayed there until just before the summer was over and the kids were preparing to go to school. I do not have to tell you how hard it was for me to leave my aunty and "uncle dad". I cried and the tears just kept running. It seemed like a dam had broken and I could not fix it. My brother had gone numb, I guess, when my father left us on that farm alone. He was never the same after that. I heard an adult say one day, "It's a shame that man messed up that kid's mind, but one day the Lord only knows he will come around." Too young to understand, I just listened and said to myself, "My brother is fine, he is safe now." My brother then took ill. He became very sick at my mother's sister's house. They said he had a very high fever and had to be taken to town to the doctor. I cried to go because we had never been apart all those years, but I could not go. I was very afraid for him. He looked bad.

Later that afternoon, which seemed like years had passed, my mother's sister returned home but without my brother. Oh, my life stood still. "Where was my brother and what did you creeps do to him?", I said to myself. I asked where my brother was and they looked at me and told me he was at the hospital, sick with worms. They said if he couldn't pass the worms he might not make it. My aunt's husband saw how upset I was and told his oldest daughter to take me out to town with her (they went shopping for food every Saturday). I wanted to stay there to hear about my brother, so I said, "No, I want to stay here." I knew my "uncle dad" would come to see about my brother and I just waited. I told myself he would be there real soon and my brother would come home. I wanted to go back to live with them because I did not like these people.

My "uncle dad" never showed up but my mother made it in very late that night. She had her boyfriend with her. She told my uncle that they had left Connecticut two hours after she got the call that my brother was very ill. Speaking of her boyfriend, she said, "He just dropped everything he had to do, called his job, and here we are." I think she was trying to show her family that she had found a good man for herself and her kids. Who knows? As you can see, because of the things I had experienced at such a young age, I had begun to develop into a very mature child. I stayed around the older kids and adults all the time. My mother came into the backroom where we all slept and hugged her little two girls. One was sleeping beside me and the other was in the bed with my oldest brother. She only made eye contact with me and waved her hands. After leaving me for almost two whole years, all I got was a wave. I felt left out from that very moment on. Thankfully, I had the hugs of my "uncle dad" and aunt on my dad's side to keep me warm.

Early that morning when I woke up my mother had already gone to the hospital to see my brother. I was so glad when they returned that evening to learn that he was doing better. The fever was going down and he was responding to his medication. As soon as he started to pass some of those worms he could come home, and I could not wait. My mother stayed with us until my brother got out of the hospital. Then she prepared to bring all of us back with her. She had to get shot records, school records and everything. This is where I began to be more of a problem for her. I had no record of even being born. The midwife never sent the papers in to the Greeneville County clerk's office. I never had all my shots, which, unfortunately, was my "uncle dad" and aunt's fault. My mother was upset, saying that she was pressed for time, her boyfriend had to get back to work and nothing was going right when it came to me. I heard some very hurtful things come out of her mouth like, "That gal's been a problem to me since before she was even born. I should leave her a__ with her people and let them take care of her since they love her so much." My aunt said, "Don't you leave your children down here. Take them all back with you. What is wrong with you? That gal belongs with her brothers and sisters. They have all suffered since you been up north. Take your children and start a life up there with them." I remember those words because if her sister had not said anything she might have left me down south with my father's people. When my brother had gotten out of the hospital, my mother got spiteful and would not let my uncle and aunt come by to see my brother because they had threatened to call the County police on her for leaving us down there and not checking on us or my other brother and sisters.

I said earlier that something had happened for her to be coming down there to get us. I just had not heard what it was until the day my dad's sister ran into my mother's twin sister that had my oldest brother and younger sisters. My dad's sister asked how the other children were doing and when was the last time she had heard from my mother. She was told that she had not heard from my mother in about four or five months. My aunt had not heard from her either and thought it was a shame that my mother went north and forgot about us. It was said that my mother had turned into a party animal and was just having the time of her life while everybody else dealt with her responsibilities. If she did not want all these children she should not have had them by all these men. So my aunt said that if she did not hurry up and come see about "these two right here that I got" she was going to call the law on my mother "and you can tell her I said so the next time you hear from her." So this is why my mother came to get us. Because my dad's sister had threatened to call the law on my mother, she was very angry at her and was mean to her when it came time for us to say goodbye. She let us say goodbye to them, but lied about sending us back in the summer to visit, even though my "uncle dad" said he would send for us or drive to get us.

Life After The Move Up North

We came up north on the Greyhound bus. We were all holding hands with my stepfather and my mother. The bus ride was long and quiet. Mom must have had much on her mind, now that I think about it. But I don't want to get ahead of myself. We changed buses in Washington, D.C. After that we finally arrived in Stamford, CT. The street we lived on was very busy with cars coming and going at a very fast pace. We were all told that the cars had no time to stop for us so we'd better not step out in the street unless we could see our way clear of the moving cars. That was our city training about the streets.

Entering the apartment we were told who was sleeping with whom. I had to sleep with my three younger sisters. These were my mother's instructions: "You better not roll over on my baby, do you hear me? And I want you to make sure this room is kept clean, do you hear me?" "Yes," I answered. "Not only this room," she said, "but the front room, the bathroom, the kitchen, and your brother's room. But do not put your butt in my room, none of you kids." I had never picked up a broom. I was always told that I was too little. At my uncle's house the older girls did the housework; my little cousin and I only played house. Now, here I was in Connecticut, away from all who loved me and could help me learn to be an adult or housekeeper or a mother or a live in babysitter at six years old. Life began to move fast for me at this early learning stage.

It was time to get registered for school. My brother and I had been apart for long periods of time only when he went to school and that time when he was in the hospital. My mother could not get me into school because my birth records had not yet been cleared. It was as if I had been hatched instead of born. I had not felt life or experienced anything until something traumatic happened. Then I felt alive. Otherwise, I just existed from day to day. Do not get me wrong. I knew I was alive at my "uncle dad" and aunt's house. I just had never connected emotionally with anyone but my brother. He was the light of my life. It seemed like we had invaded other people lives or were just out there with no real connection to anyone. Well, back to getting into school. The clinic where you got your physical sent a letter home saying I needed to be taken to the city clinic to get a vaccine before entering school. As soon as they heard from the North Carolina clerk's office I could start school.

Everything concerning me was getting my mother very stressed out. My stepfather kept encouraging her by telling her that these thing take time. As time went on I did get into school, although I was a month behind. My mother was told not to worry about me but to make sure the other little ones' paper work and shots were up to date so that they would be prepared when it came time for them to start school. Winter came and I began to get sick: high fevers, sore throats, out of school a lot. I hated this because all I did when I was home was to play "fetch-it": go get this and bring me that; put this up; find me that. All day long. I hated getting sick, so I tried to stay in school and not tell anyone. But high fevers, as you know, make you very weak. So, I had to either stay home or get sent home. My stepfather would leave work, pick me up from school, drop me off at home and go back to work. This made my mother angry because she thought I was costing him money. But it wasn't a problem for him. All he did was ask his boss if he could run to the school, get me, and come right back. He was a good man, friend and worker. My mother was the problem. She was mean just like her sisters. Boy, what hateful women, I thought.

One day I came home from school and all the curtains were off the window. That's when I found out we were moving, just like that. Oh, my heart hurt because of my nice teachers and neighborhood friends. We moved all the way across town to a really loud neighborhood with more blacks than the neighborhood we had just left. I later learned that we had moved into the ghetto. There were drinking parties every weekend starting on Thursday night and lasting until Sunday. Some neighbors had people over for drinks or house parties to make rent money. I learned my mother attended these parties while my stepfather stayed at home with us. She would come in late, all drunk. He would put her to bed some nights. I would hear him pleading with her to stop staying out and drinking until she had to be brought home. He did not mind her enjoying herself but he reminded her that she had children to look after. He would say, "I'm here to try and help you like I gave you my word I would, but you got to do also." Sometimes she must have fallen asleep on him because I would hear him in the kitchen. During those times I would get up and go to the bathroom just to make sure he was OK. He would sometimes ask me if everything was alright with the girls and I would tell him yes and go back into the room. Sometimes I would ask for something to drink. Iced tea was my favorite. It was real sweet, but we could not have it late at night because the girls would wet the bed but not me.

We lived in a very violent neighborhood. I started to seeing men beating on women like they were crazy. Nose bleeds, black eyes, busted lips. Just bruised up. Then the cops would come and take the man away and the woman would go get him from jail. The neighborhood seemed to be getting worse and so did my mother's drinking. My stepfather began to complain and argue with her right in front of us kids. He was getting fed up, but he loved my mother. Well, one day after he got paid he came and gave her some money and took all his stuff and left. My mother took this out on me and started beating me, saying she hated me and that she wished she had killed me when she had the chance. She always made these statement when she got very upset or scared I believe. I was born early - a premature six month old. I did not know that until I got older, but I looked back years ago on these very words and I truly believe she tried to abort me, but I survived. The reason I say this is I was the only early child she had and only small child in weight. This woman's babies were born weighing 9-10 pounds.

I think my stepfather stayed gone for three weeks. I would sneak by his job and tell him to please come back, that we would be good. But he would say that it wasn't us, that "your mother and I just need some time apart." I did not understand, but I was seven years old then. When he finally came back he brought all kinds of goodies with him. Then he told us to go outside and play. I looked right at my mother because if she looked wrong I was not going to disrespect him because

I cared a lot for him but not enough to get a whipping. When it came to whippings this lady had no mercy on me. When she whipped me she would throw soda glass bottles, pots and shoes upside my little head. It did not matter. I felt she was trying to kill me every time she beat me. She yelled at my brothers and sister once in a while because they were still little, but man did she burn my little behind up. I got a beating every other day, if not everyday. She only communicated to me with verbal abuse and her ironing cord or rope. I have scars on my body from her beatings that I will take to my grave. Many scars from her, others from my own adult life mistakes.

We went out to play so my mother and stepfather had the house to themselves. I guess they were making up. The next thing you know we had to move again. I came home from school and the house was emptied out. My mother, stepfather and my two brothers and a neighbor of theirs moved us. Where was everybody and where were all of our things? Boy, I got scared. I was too young to keep going through that sort of trauma. "Mama, where are you?" I cried. Where were my brothers? I began to cry as fear gripped my heart. I remembered what my "uncle dad" made me promise - to take of my brother. I called out his name. My sister was with me on the porch and she was crying because I was so upset. I held on to her real tight and told her everything was going to be alright.

It was about that time that a neighbor was coming up the street with a brown bag in her hand. She said my mother had asked her to keep an eye on us until she took the last load of our things to the house. House?! What house?! I looked at that lady and said, "We are moving again?" She said, "Yes, your mama said she was going to need a bigger place. She has some good news for you girls as well," and she laughed. A truck came around the corner not long after this neighbor had rescue me. My brother got out of the truck first since he was sitting close to the door. He looked like a proud young man when he saw me looking at him in that big truck. My heart settled down once I saw him. I told him later how he had scared me to death and he told me to stop being silly. We were there with my mother for good and he wasn't going to leave me. I looked at him and I felt his words; they made me feel safe again. I was not pleased to be living with her, but at least I knew he and I would always be together.

Unknowing to us, my mother was pregnant at the time she and my stepfather got back together. Everyone was happy except me. It just meant that I had one more baby to deal with. I had just gotten these other two off of bottles and out of diapers. I don't want to sound like I'm complaining but from the time I arrived in Connecticut I had to take care of the girls as well as clean and mop, while my stepfather cooked. All the women in the apartment building where we lived used to talk about how well-trained my mother had my stepfather, how he would bring his paycheck home and give it to her before he cashed it. They would laugh about how she was "taking care of business." Then they would talk about us, her children, and how we had the apartment sparkling clean at all times and how she beat me. They would say, "Girl, you make my skin crawl the way you hit that child sometimes. I'm not getting in your business but you may not need to whip her so much. She is a good child. Just may need a little directing every now and then, but not every day. No child is that bad." That's when the laughter stopped. My mother got mad and started cursing at those women. But they were not lying. There have been others over the years who would say the same words to her.

The baby finally came and she was a pretty little thing. Another girl. Five girls now and two boys, seven kids altogether. I believe my mother was around thirty years old at the time. The new baby did become my responsibility, just like I knew she would, but my stepfather and oldest brother helped me out. She brought joy in the house for the first year, then one day I came home from school to find that she had been taken to the hospital for seizures. No one knew why she had these seizures, but my mother blamed my stepfather. She would say that his family had diseases and he would say that my mother was crazy and that the child was just born sickly. There was a lot of whispering among the adults, but I never got to learn clearly what was going on. WHY? Because we moved yet again, this time to Bridgeport, CT.

We moved to another ghetto. More blacks and kids EVERYWHERE! I needed some peace and quiet like I had when we lived down south. Unfortunately, that seemed like a dead dream. I did not hear from my uncle and aunt at all. They promised to write but nothing ever came. I thought maybe they did write, but we kept moving so they may not have had the address. We moved so much.

I know by now people might wonder how I, as a child, survived everything that had happened to me up to this point. I was told that my grandfather on my mother's side was a preacher. I never really knew him, but I do remember him being there with me on the day my mother left us to move to Connecticut. He was standing on the porch with me and as she was pulling off I began to cry. He said, "Don't worry baby. You are going to be alright. You are going to do just fine." He placed his hands on my head. Moments later that big old shiny black car came up the road to pick up my brother and me. We were going to live with my uncle and aunt. By my grandfather being a preacher, I suppose he prayed and asked God to keep a hedge of protection around all his grandchildren. You know God is a keeper. My mother had a friend whose daughter used to take me to church with her. I loved going because I got out of doing the housework and I could rest my mind for a moment. I gave my life to the Lord one Easter Sunday. I had on a pretty green dress. When they had the altar call, my family friend went up and she grabbed me by my hands and pulled me up there with her. My mother did not give me permission to do anything but to sit in church and behave myself, or else I would not be allowed to go again. Because going to church got me out of the house, I was going to behave.

So that Easter Sunday I was adopted into the King's family. No matter what I did or went through God brought me out even when I did not fully understand salvation. I was seven years old then I believe. Once I received the Lord in my life He said He would never leave me nor forsake me. God is still faithful to His word because even then he kept me. My grandfather must have prayed for angels to surround all of us as well because back there on that farm that man in the bright white shirt and those kids had to be angles sent by God to save us from going to sleep that Christmas Eve night and freezing to death. I tell you God has been with me even when I did not know him. I believe that on that porch that day, when my grandfather placed his hands on my head he transferred what was on him to me. I never saw him after that day on the porch. He went home to be with the Lord when I was just nine years old.

Now, back to the move to Bridgeport. I found out we moved to Bridgeport so my little sister could be near the specialist she needed. I could accept that. We moved to an apartment that was over a bar named The Johnson. Man, they had loud music every weekend. It was a very fancy place so it was only open from Thursday to Sunday night. The people that came to this bar did not start fights there. They were well-behaved at the bar, but the men took their wives home and beat them. I knew this because I would see the scars the next day. Across the street was a restaurant, a pool hall, a numbers joint, a barber shop and a drug store. I share this because I made a lot of runs to the store and restaurant for my mother and her friends. Also, the A&P grocery store was underneath us as well. I had my days cut out for me.

Our new neighbors were three sisters, two of them married and living with their families. The youngest sister lived with the oldest. She had just moved from the south to get a better job. The sisters took to me. Directly across from us lived a lady that had this funny laugh. She lived with her sons and one daughter, who she was my little sister's age. This lady had a big fat boyfriend who was the father of her kids, but they had never gotten married. Upstairs was another lady who lived with her son next door to the sister on the top floor. Then there was an empty apartment that was used Thursday through Sunday nights for after-hours gambling and selling of alcohol. This was run by our neighbor across the street.

My stepfather was still living with us as well. He looked after us as if we were his own kids. But my sister who was born right after me hated his guts. Why? I do not know. My mother always told my sister to listen to my oldest brother when she went out without my stepfather, who, like I said before, did not drink like my mother. She drank like a fish every day. My mother had to have a bottle. It seemed like everybody in the building drank, but not like my mother. My mother was on welfare and she had my stepfather living with us so she could collect welfare and get his check too. Welfare workers use to come visit once a month and we had to clean the house like the president was on the way. My stepfather had always given my mother his paycheck. He did not cash it until he came home and picked her up to go with him. He took us out to eat at White Castle in White Plains, NY. We went on long Sunday drives. He had a nice Cadillac. It was pretty and big with these long, pointed fins in the back. Then there was a bird on the hood. Boy, that car was nice. He was a driver for a tire company that allowed him to transfer to the Bridgeport location when we moved.

The school was only four blocks up the street. My mother could hang out the window and watch us walk to school. Like I shared earlier, my neighbors all loved me. They all needed me to go here, run there, clean this and that. My mother did not mind, seeing that they were paying me. It was during this time that my little sister's seizures seemed to go away. She outgrew them, the doctor said. I did a lot of babysitting for neighbors but could not stay overnight. My stepfather did not approve of that, thank God. The beatings from my mother continued, but not so much around him. School was tough for my next youngest sister and me. We both were built like brick houses. We had butts. Man, if we did not have anything else we had our mama's shape. We were definitely her daughters, people would say. She would just laugh. My mother was a very pretty, well-built woman. I was very pretty, as well. However, my mother was not the one to tell me that. I heard it from the men that we walked past on the way to school. I would run home.

Whenever my mother got upset about something I forgot to do or did not do it right she made sure to tell me that I was no good just like my red, no good daddy. Day in and day out. She made me mad, telling me that I never would be anything. I just wanted to go home to my father for some sick reason. I just felt close to him. I used to daydream that he would come and get me and I would never have to see her again. This man had left me and my brother in a farm house while he was in an alcoholic black out. But which one was worse? At least he was not there to beat me everyday. My stepdad would tell me, "Do not let what your mama says hurt you. You are a good kid and you are going to do fine." Those were the same words her dad spoke to me on the porch that day. Confirmation, but of course I did not know that then. I went to school many days with whelps on my back, my body aching, dry tears running down my face because I could not let the teachers know. The whelps used to sting while we played kickball on the playground. Another student would get shoved to the ground real hard by me only because they hit me on the back too hard and I was already hurting. In school I was labeled as a violent student, a bully. I just hurt and wanted to be left alone. Nobody seemed to see my life of pain. If they did they were too afraid to stand up to my mother and speak up for me.

Eventually, my mother had another baby, a boy. I was tired of cleaning baby butts and I prayed, "Lord, I sure hope no more comes after this one." Well, no more babies came because my mother could not have any more. My little brother was born with brain damage due to her drinking too much while she was pregnant with him. He had seizures just like my little sister, but much worse. Every other night we were at the hospital with him. His brain ached some kind of bad. I can only imagine. My mother could not handle this at all. It was at this time that my stepfather left her for good. She became so depressed and mean. I thought she was going to beat the skin off of me. I used to bleed from my whelps and she did not care. One day she hit me in the top of my head with a shoe heel, a red one at that, and knocked a hole in my head. I was bleeding, but this women did not care. The more abusive she became with me the more violent I became out in the streets. I was not going to get beat at home *and* in the streets. So, brother, if you came after me, you got it. I fought like I had lost my mind. I had become my mother, but I felt bad after I did what I did. However, my mother did not feel. She hurt and wanted to get rid of the pain.

One day the neighbor downstairs came to the door and yelled out my mother's name and she said, "If you hit that child one more time I will call the police right now. Hit her again. It don't make no sense you beating that child like that everyday. It don't make no sense. No child is that darn bad. This child do all she can to help you. Hit her again. I'm not scared of you. The other's maybe, but I'm not. Now hit her one more time today and see if I don't call the police." This was music to my ears. My mother started cursing and then told me to get the hell out and go live with them since they have so much to tell me to do. I wanted to go, but I was afraid. The lady told me, "Come down. Here. I'll keep you right here with my kids, and when we eat you'll eat. My kids sleep you will sleep, too." I went downstairs. I was so afraid I was shaking as my mother said, "Get down there 'fore I throw your a___ down there."

My brother was playing football at the park and I did not want to leave him, no way. My uncle-dad said we are to stay together. I went downstairs as I was told. I was scared, but not of them because I did a lot of babysitting for them. I was scared of my mother. That woman had lost her mind giving me away. My neighbor and her husband later went and talked with my mother. I only know what they told me. I would be staying with them for a while but I had to go home to my mom's house everyday after school and in the mornings to help get the kids off and home from school.

My brother and I had a talk. I thought he would be upset, but he wasn't. He said that family cared for me a lot and now he wouldn't have to worry so much about me getting beatings all the time. My brother loved me very much. He just stayed out of the house because he could not handle me getting mistreated. My sister next to me got beat, too, but not like I did because everybody told my mom how much she looked like her and was built like her. She was my mother's eyeball and my older brother was the wind beneath her wings. She really loved him. My oldest brother had it made; he got the best of everything. The clothing he wore was top of the line. His hair always looked good because he stayed at the barbershop getting his hair processed. The rest of us wore clothes people gave us or that my mother went to the thrift store and bought. We always got new underclothes. Because we were girls, she was a stickler about our hygiene. When I babysat I would steal money from people, layaway some school clothes at the nickel and dime store, and than get them out. My biological brother was a rough neck and he only wanted to play football, so he really needed sneakers and knee pants or slacks for the school year.

My mother did not mistreat my brother. I guess she had approval from my dad to keep him seeing that he was a boy and it was less trouble to have a boy around than a girl. Girls are a bigger responsibility, I suppose. My mother was hard on me. I do not care what anyone reading this book may feel or think. You should have been there to take some of those beatings everyday. Then tell me what your opinion would be. I loved my mother. I always wanted her to kiss me on my forehead in the morning before I left for school just like the other kids' moms did them. She would just tell me to "get my butt down them stairs to school. I'll give you a kiss but you isn't going to like it when I give it to you." She would laugh it off and I would just turn and leave. This did something to me. It left a hole in my heart. I tried to kiss her more than once, but the hole in my heart got bigger. I finally gave up on it; it just was not going to happen.

When I moved downstairs my life changed. No beatings. I did my homework then I went upstairs to my mom's to do what I had to do. This was heaven, but only for two months. My mother got sick real bad.

She kept saying that when she got to New York she would be all right. This did not make sense, going to New York to see a doctor. Why would her doctor be in New York? That was a long way to go to the doctor. I was young so it did not occur to me at that age that my mother believed in root doctors. This was the kind of doctor, I learned later, that she was talking about going to. I believed she had planned this fake sickness so I would move back home. She looked ok to me. She still yelled all the time. This is when my life really gets turned upside down.

My mother, her friend next door, and her friend from Stamford got together and planned a house party to raise money to pay their bills and to have extra money for themselves. The party was to be at my mother's house. This way she would get the biggest cut of the money. She did not want her friends to know about her belief in roots. Now, shouldn't that tell you something was wrong with this kind of doctor? Anyway, we got the house all cleaned up and I started helping them prep for the house party. Man, they worked my little body down that weekend, but my life took another turn. It was Friday night and all the people started coming in and the drinks start selling along with the food. More people, more drinks, on and on and on.

We finally sold out of everything and people had to go. My mother said she had to put her children to bed. We had been up since we got up for school that morning. This tall man asked to use the bathroom before he left the party. He was drunk. I can't remember how long he had been at the party but he should have known where the bathroom was. He said, "Show me to the little boys room, baby," and he laughed, looking at me. I looked right at my mother. She told me to show him and then she started to clean up the kitchen. So I wouldn't have to cut through the rooms where the other kids were, I proceeded to escort this bum down the hall to the bathroom. He looked back, and when he did not see anyone behind us he reached out to touch my butt. That scared me. He said, "Don't worry. I won't hurt you. I'm here to help out your mama and you kids." Then he touched my chest. I said, "Do not put your hands on me again or I will tell my stepfather on you." But he just laughed. He knew my stepfather had left, I guess, like all the other neighbors did. "Here baby," he said, "I'm here to help you and you help me. I'll keep money in your little piggy bank." He handed me three dollars and I think I got scared. He pushed the money in my hands and said, "You children are the reason your mother stays so upset. Do what you're supposed to do to help her and maybe she won't be so mean to you. Besides that, who's going to believe you over a grown man like Mr. _____? Now get in that kitchen before your mama comes looking for you." He then touched me again on my butt and laughed. I hated to hear people laugh. I did not find anything in life that would cause me to laugh.

I did as I was told and started toward the kitchen. Now I was nine years old going on ten when I first got touched. I wanted to tell my mother, but every time I started to form the words in my mind fear of getting beaten for lying scared me more than what he did. I didn't think she would believe me. I became very afraid to be around any of her company. I felt if I stayed out of sight she would not call me to do anything for them so I used to hide underneath the bed when she had company. Even the women would just want to talk about how much my sister and I were built like our mother and touch our butts. They were not doing anything to me but I just could not trust anyone to touch me. Her male crew began to grow. There were more men than ever coming to our house. Before you could tell that the head of our house, the covering at that time, was a female who drank, my mother had close men friends who would come over and bring a bottle and a bag of food telling her they had a taste for some porgies. Nobody could fry fish like her, boy, I tell you. The men would say, "Fry these up for me and here's some chicken for the kids. Take this ten dollars for using your gas. I know you can use this during the week for the children." Mama would laugh and say, "I had a taste for some fresh porgies a day or so ago," and head for the kitchen. My mother did not want any kind of food in her house unless it was fresh. She must have had food poison once and thought someone had put roots on her. Well, it happens when you let your mind wander. It picks up something stupid to make sense out of something you have not medically experienced before.

They would laugh and drink while she cooked. I would get touched when she was not looking because she seemed to always want me around her and these men. I would go get what she wanted and head back under my bed. I lived under my bed. I loved the cool floor and it seem so quiet under there. I had to go one day to drop off some number slips for my mother at this man's house and she told me not to go into his house for any reason. So when I arrived at the door I rang the bell. He came to the door and I handed him the number slip. He told me my mother wanted me on the phone. I said, "No she don't. She told me not to come into your house and I'm not." He then said, "I will tell her what you said and when she beats that tail of yours then you will know for sure who is lying." Beat me? Oh boy, I got scared and I ran to take the phone. He locked the door behind me and I could not get past him to leave his house. He weighed a good three hundred pounds or more. He pulled my shorts down and kept trying to get me on the bed, but I had a good struggle going on. I would slide from his gripping hold, trying to find that little what ever he planned to stick in me. He was just too fat to hold me. I got loose and I told him, "I'm going to scream and tell every body in the neighborhood what you are trying to do to me if you don't open that door now." I started screaming. Boy, could I yell. He said, "Ok. Don't you tell a soul about this, you hear me?" I said, "Open that door now!" He let me go. I could not tell my mother what had happened. She was already yelling at me for playing after she had sent me to do something and not coming right back. "Just look at how sweaty and musty you are," she said. "Go get in that tub! I should tear your behind up right now." I said to myself that I would not try that not right now. I was still a little bit unstable after having to fight that big fat man off of me.

Something was going on with my mother and the trips to New York that she and my oldest brother would take. Then the house parties and the men touching me. The ones she considered her friends always brought a bag of food with them and a few bucks to help her through the week. She would send my sister and me food shopping on check day to the larger super market. I would sit in the middle. I did not want their creepy hands on my sister. We got money, a dollar or two, for me being touched. She did not know what they were doing. It started to be a game for me. I would walk around them, look at them, take their money and run. Then I stared to be the one to laugh at them because now what could they do to me. They were the ones that would need to explain why they gave me money without asking my mother first. That was an unspoken rule in those days. No man gave money to your kids without your permission. So now I used this hurt for my own gain.

I turned ten years old and, boy, my body was really hot to look at. The men would tell me. My mother did not allow me to walk to the store or play in the yard. The very thing she tried to protect me from was going on in our home. She meant well but it was a little too late. Now, I had been molested but not raped. In the midst of all this I loved my mother. Again, do not get it ill. She was just an alcoholic who men took advantage of in their own sly way. I tried to tell her, "Mom, do not let these men keep coming over here. Let them party next door sometimes. They're always coming over here. We never get to bed until late every single weekend." I felt my mother looking at me but she did not answer me. The next week there was no company. She went next door. This was great. One weekend I heard loud fussing and I ran out onto the porch. It was this short dark-skinned man and my mother. The man yelled, "You gon' tell me tonight who you want - me or him - or I'm going to split your lip." I called for my brothers to help. I grabbed a kitchen knife and handed one to my brother, but he drop it (the chicken). We went on the back porch and stood next to our mother. My brother said, "Man, what you threatening our mama for?" He said, "You kids go on back in the house. This is not kids business." I said, "It is if you talking about hurting our mama. It is all our business." He looked at me with the knife in my hand and said, "What you going to do with that?" I said, "You'll find out if you hit my mother, I tell you that much."

I moved closer to my mother and she said, "Put that knife down. He's not going to do anything to me but get his a____ down them stairs." Our neighbor, my godfather, came running upstairs by that time. "What is going on up here," he said. "Man, leave that women and her kids alone. Come down here and lets you and me talk like two grown adults about this. You have had too much to drink. Tomorrow you'll regret this whole mess." Then the man walked off with my godfather (It was his family that I stayed with for two months). My family and the neighbor next door laughed and talked about me not being afraid to stand up for my mother and wanted to know who taught me how to use a knife. My mother just looked at me and I said, "Nobody is going to hurt my mother. Nobody." I later found out she was playing the role with this man and some other creep, just for money. Every time he showed up the other jerk showed up, too. They both were just too old for my mother. She was very pretty, but losing it slowly. Gaining a lot of weight and just drinking.

Well, if you think things changed between my mother and me you are sadly mistaken. She felt that I was getting too grown and needed to sit my fast tail down some where. This is what I got for coming to her rescue. I do believe, now that I am grown, that maybe she responded that way to keep me in check so I would not come after her. I don't know. She just was not thrilled about me and the knife. But her boys coming to her rescue was all she talked about. For me, it did not matter. I loved her and no one was going to hurt her. Not around me. She just did not know how much I really loved her.

My sister was her eyeball, so I continued in the background of the family and stayed underneath my bed reading until I was needed. I was still a virgin only in physical form. My mind had been raped, my spirit had been raped. I was emotionally damaged and scarred. Nobody put their hands on me or I was going to kill them. Hurt had taken over my life. Violence and destruction was my last name in the streets. Nobody bothered me in school. I took kids' lunch money. Black or white, I did not care about your color just the color of your money. I was not raised to look at a person's skin color. Remember, I came from Stamford. Black and white kids stayed together and we played together. Only when I moved to Bridgeport did a person's color matter.

I had now shut down from everyone and everything. I stole all the time from people I babysat for. They knew my mother was taking the money they paid me and drinking it up. I would clean houses every Saturday, along with doing my own house work, and she would take that money. I would lie sometimes and say they only paid me this much just to be able to put money on my layaway for school. She smoked Winston cigarettes. I used to have to stay up at night waiting for her to fall asleep to take the cigarette out of her hands so she would not burn up herself or the rest of us. Man, I loved my mom. She became like a little child to me that I had to protect and look after. Many nights I would hear her walking the floor and praying. She said her father always taught them to pray and that with God all things are possible. She believed in Him but she did not live like He was able to help her. However, God always managed to provide food for our mouths. She would say she didn't know how she was going to pay the insurance man, but He made a way. At the time I did not know she was talking about the Lord. Anyway, I would get up and peep to see who she was talking to and go back to bed. There was no one there that I could see. She did this so much, but I was not concerned. She was not hurting herself.

I can remember being ten or eleven years old and running errands for the madam that ran the stable right across the street from us. On Thursday, Friday and Saturday I would have to go pickup her order of sodas and juices from the A&P. This woman taught me how to play a man for what he was worth, not what he said he had. She taught me how she got started in her type of business. A stable is a place where you house prostitutes. They sell their bodies for money and the madam gets a fee from the proceeds. She said that she would go down to the train station or bus station and wait for the girls who were coming from down South to work as sleep-in girls for the white folks. Sometimes the husbands in these white families were the main ones that wanted you to come live-in so he could make you his sex slave. It did not happen all the time, but it happened often enough to where she had built her own stable full of southern girls. She said if a white man came to the bus station to pick you up for his wife and he knew what you were wearing and you did not look pleasing to him, he just left you right at the station and would tell his wife that you did not show up. The poor girl would just be stuck in a strange town and her pride would not allow her to go back home, not after her parents had given all they had to send her up there. Also keeping her from going back home was the memory of working in those hot fields. The girls would take this madam's offer until they felt they could do better on their own or until a john would promise them a better life than what she was willing to offer them. Most of the time they ended up being "pimped out" by a man who now beats them and takes their money. I used to see a lot of that, too. I felt so sorry for those girls that would let men beat them for not making enough money for him that night. They used to beat them with these small baseball bats. The madam said that at least her girls knew they were safe from that kind of life.

By the time I was twelve years old my little brother was placed in a school for children with cerebral palsy. We were told that he had severe muscle and nerve damage and would never walk and probably gain very little, if any, speech. He would not ever be normal, but he could learn -

and so could we - how to deal with his disability. My mother could not handle this truth and she drank more. One day, after my little brother had us up all night and day for about a week, my mother just threw him. He went flying across the bed grasping for air as she threw him. I sensed something and was on my way into her room anyway. As he landed on the bed, I told her, "Mama, I will take him and you get some sleep." Speaking about the hospital she said, "They are going to get this baby on the right meds or keep him until they do." She had snapped and needed some help herself. Drinking was not making this reality go away. She was angry at his dad (my stepfather) for leaving her after this boy was born. He did not stick around to help out. She hurt so bad. I stopped getting angry at her when she beat me and called me names. I just took it the best I could. I hardly ever cried any more. Sometimes, I would get alone and look at the many scars and I would break down, but not in front of her. I would not even let her see me cry. This made her angry, too. It hurt, but I wasn't going to cry any more tears for what I could not stop.

I stopped looking at her because she thought I would be rolling my eyes at her and I did, from time to time. She had a bad habit of punching and slapping me in my face, leaving red marks. Kids could see them at school, so I did not look people in the face. No need in it. I used to volunteer at my brother's school when I could. I also attended his school meetings. My mother was "out to lunch" and she just could not handle much more. Someone told her about seeing the family doctor for help. I did not know she was prescribed pills. Valium and black beauties, we used to call them. It was this very small light-green pill and a long black pill. When she took these she smiled, did house work, cooked and baked for us, like she did when we first came to live with her.

She cooked good meals. We never went hungry, even when my stepfather left us. Once, when we lived in Stamford, we had no food. Boy, I remember that like it happened last week. We were out of food and my mom had run up her store credit. It had snowed and she was looking out the window. She may have been crying, but I don't know. She told my brothers to get up and shovel the snow. "We need money," she said. I wanted to go with them but she wouldn't let me. Girls weren't supposed to shovel snow. "No one sends girls out to shovel snow," she said. "Who would know I'm a girl, mama. I look just like him and my head will be covered." She laughed and said, "Girl, get out of here. I don't care. Ask your brothers." I ran in the boys room and said, "Mama said I can go too if you say it's ok." My older brother said, "Go sit down. What girl do you see shoveling snow? None. Sit your tomboy butt down." He was the oldest so I just looked at my brother. He said, "Don't look at me." I told him he was just jealous that I'll make more money then him. He heard me and said, "Yeah, sure. I'm a man." I responded, "No you're not. You're a short punk." He was shorter than my brother and me, but not that much. "No, girl. That snow is cold and heavy. You'll be crying to come back not even an hour after you get out there. Who do you think is going to turn around just to bring you back?" I begged and begged until my brother looked at my oldest brother and said, "Let her go this time. When she sees how cold it is and we don't come right back, she won't want to go anymore."

He let me go and mother told him to make sure he held my hand. I was freezing not even an hour after we left, but I was so excited about being out with my brother and helping out that I hardly even felt the cold. I did not do much shoveling, either, but every body thought I was Kirby, their little brother under that hat and they gave me money. I got money just for being out there trying to shovel with my big brothers. It began to get dark and my mother needed to get food so we started home. I had so much money. When mama saw us coming she opened the door and started telling us how worried she was. She asked us how we did. My brothers said, "We did most of the work and she got money for being the 'little brother.' Them dummies did not know she was a girl." I said, "I told you I look like him under a hat. They did not know the difference." We made over one hundred dollars. After that day I was allowed to shine shoes with my brother and he did not mind me going. So I have worked all my life doing something to help our household survive.

I stared taking pills at school in the seventh grade. We used to purchase them for fifty cents a piece. Some of the eighth-grade boys sold them. I would get them by taking off some of the white girls for their lunch money. Then I started selling them myself and getting my pills free. Man, it did not matter what my mom did or said to me. I felt nothing at all. I kept my grades up in school and I just stayed high. She did not know it but I stayed high every single day. She would not let me leave her sight, afraid, I guess, that someone was going to touch me. Sorry, but that had happened already. Don't get me wrong. She was doing what any mother would do to protect her fine, well-built daughter. I had inherit her "junk in my trunk", as they say. I became out of control at school, fighting all the time, cursing out the teacher. Just bad. But I really did not mean to say and do the things I was doing. I just kept losing control of my temper. I felt like two different people living in the same body. The real me was very quiet and shy, the one that liked to stay under the bed and read. Then the other person inside of me - you could not talk to her. She just did not listen. She stayed on the defense all the time, fighting and cursing and getting into trouble.

My mother saw that I was becoming a problem so she started giving me more house work to do. Anything to keep me in the house. That was not working any more because I was fed up with everything and every body. Life owed me nothing and I was not looking for anything or anybody. I never hated anyone but I did used to pray that God would let me die or to kill my mother. I used to wish I was dead all the time. I started doing things just for the attention. No other reason. I would fight, steal, lie; it did not matter. In my mind, I was just out there only because my mother would not take her feet off of my neck. If she could keep me in the house, she did. Every Saturday all I did was clean the house, the floors, the stove, the walls, the beds, the windows. I did this every single weekend, along with cleaning neighbors' bathrooms and kitchens, and cleaning silver for her friends for the cheap price of three dollars. Nobody needed to clean as much as my mother had us cleaning. We painted the whole house twice a year like we were painters.

I hated it, yes I did. I'm getting angry even now writing about some of the stupid things she had me to do. It only made me more rebellious toward everybody. I used to pray, "God, why don't you send my daddy to get me?" But it never happened. I'm not saying I was a perfect child. What child is? But I never had a chance to live or think as a child. I just functioned and existed as if I had no right to smile, dream or play. I remember one day asking my mother in front of her girlfriend next door if I could go up the street to play with my classmate and her sister. Well, she had a fit and told me to go clean the girls' room closet and get all the clothes off the floor and hang them up properly. I heard her girlfriend say, as I was walking away, "Now, it's none of my business, but you need to start letting that child go out and play a little bit. You can't keep her shut up like that to much longer 'cause she is growing, as we both can see. She'll do fine if you start letting her out now. If not, then later on she is going to be buck wild with whatever little bit of freedom that gal gets. Then you are not going to be able to do nothing with her if she gets out there like we did."

I was listening inside the door. If she knew I was there she would have skinned me alive. Children did not listen in on grown folks' conversations. My mother's response was, "I'm going to let her out but not before her cousin gets up here. My sister's daughter is graduating from high school and she wants to come live with me to get her a job so she can help her mama out." Her friend replied, "Well that's good cause that child needs to get out more." By the way, I hated going to this friend's house. Her kids' father would feel my butt every time my mother sent me next door. I hated to go over there. I had to sneak in and out or make a loud noise so her girlfriend would know that I was in the house. He touched me until they moved away. Boy, was I glad to see that fat man leave that building. Why does it seem to always be a fat ugly man or a bald-headed man that touch children the most?

I was eleven years old when my cousin first came to live with us from down south. She was very nice looking with long curly hair. We all had long hair. Mine was thinner than my sister's but the four of us from the south had long hair, as well. This cousin seemed to be my oldest brother's favorite cousin and my mother's favorite niece. I did not remember ever seeing her, so to have a friend in the house who was our cousin as well made me feel a little more free. Now maybe she would help with the house work, as well. She was to room with the rest of us girls, and my sister next to me got to sleep on the small couch in my mother's room. You know she would have to be the one to be up with my mother eating goodies at night. You know how when no other kid is around they give you a little snack that they may be having? That was my mother and my sister.

I got along very well with this cousin. I got a chance to get out because I had to show her how to get to different stores and bus stops. We laughed and talked a lot. She took me to the park and all that kind of stuff. Man, it was nice. We did house cleaning together and she also stood up for me so I did not get so many beatings anymore. But she started this yelling and fussing thing all day long. There was this girl that my brother had been dating for a long time. So, my brother and my cousin went out at night to the girl's house together so her mother would think that my brother was walking my cousin to and from her house to visit this girl, but it was the other way around. My cousin actually was the one doing my brother a favor. They were seventeen years old but this girl was fifteen, so you know he was headed for trouble. I had not met the girl yet but I knew he had a girlfriend. My mother would have had a fit because she felt no girl was good enough for her son. She acted like he was her husband, always making sure his clothes were ironed just right, his shoes like new all the time, and his food put up for him when he got home from work. My oldest brother was like the man of the house. He worked a full time job after school and he kept us kids for my mother when she took her trips to New York to see the root doctor. Man, she saw him faithfully for many years, too. You would think that the person who told you who did what to you and what number to play in order to hit the lottery would be rich his doggone self. That was my reaction to this New York madness.

Anyway, my oldest brother helped my mother out more than anyone will ever know. He gave to her, he shared with her, he took care of us and I thank God for him. He has since gone home to be with the Lord. I know he went because I asked God to show me if he was with Him, and the Holy Spirit showed up in that service and a peace came over me. I looked at my mother and I said, "Mama, he made it in." We all praised the Lord that day. This left a smile on my mother's heart because she loved him more than life itself.

Getting back to my cousin who had come to live with us. She and my brother got along and they would stay out late, until after 11:00 pm. My mother had a rule in her house: no one came in her house after midnight. She did not care who you were. With a house full of growing kids she needed to be strict in that area. With no man in the house she had to do both jobs. My cousin took me downtown with her every weekend, and on Saturday nights she would do our hair for my mother for church. She always wanted to do things for her aunt just because she was so kind to take her. My mother enjoyed having her here, I could tell. I liked her being there as well because it had been a long time since I had been beaten by my mother. The beatings may have been ok except for what she beat us with and how often she beat us. But when my cousin came, the beatings just stopped. Man, was my body glad. She did a lot of fussing and that was ok for a while.

Now I told you my cousin was seventeen years old and my mother's favorite niece. Well, one night she came home without my brother, telling my mother that her stomach was hurting and that she was going to take a bath and go to bed. She kissed my mother on her forehead and said, "Good night. I love you." My mother did not respond; she just smiled. Man, this hurt me. She would not let me come near her to kiss her but she let my cousin do it. Boy, I felt crappy. My cousin looked at me as she walked by and she smiled. I was too young to realize what "being setup" meant, but I learned that night for sure. I sat in the doorway of our living room watching TV until I heard my mother telling me to turn the TV off and go to bed. She would sit at the living room window for hours listening to the people come and go from the club downstairs. She would either be talking to herself or to God. I did not know, but my cousin said, "All the sisters do that girl. Don't pay that no mind. My mama do it too. It's a family thing, I see now, because I thought your mother was the only one that didn't do it but I see she does it, too." I told her I had to get up early in the morning to get the kids fed and told her "good night".

I lay down on the twin bed across from her and no sooner than my mind and body started to wind down she asked me if I was asleep. "Not yet," I said. Why, Lord, why did I answer her question? She said, "You know I love you and I'll do anything for you. I keep my aunt off of you, 'cause you know she'd be beating you all everyday, especially you, if it wasn't for me keeping her off of you, right?" I said, "Yeah, I guess so. Thanks for doing that 'cause, man, she 'bout to kill me." She said, "I don't know why your mama's the way she is. When we were coming up in our house our daddy didn't let our mama beat on us like that." Then she said, "Come over here so we don't wake your mother up while we talk." I went over to where she was and sat on the side of the bed, and when I sat down she touched my chest. Boy, I froze. Man, I was flat as a pancake so now what was she grabbing at but air. I looked at her and I said, "What are you doing?" She said, "I'm going to teach you how to get some breasts." I said, "I don't want any right now." I was scared but too afraid to yell for my mother. This was her favorite niece.

Then she took my hand and stuck it between her legs. I immediately started pulling my hand away. She could tell I was scared so she let go and said, "I'm not going to touch you but this is what I want from you every night. It helps me to sleep. It keeps me happy. Don't you want me to be happy so I can keep your mother off of your butt?" I felt numb and confused all at once.

Now my stomach was starting to hurt. I was getting sick behind just the thought of this mess. I was like, "Wait a minute. Slow down world or hurry up life and let me catch a hold of what I'm really supposed to do here. First, the men - fat, drunk, old, stinking - touching me and now this woman - my cousin - wanting me to have sex with her. I'm eleven years old world. Hello? This has gone too far. Wake me up, Lord. This is not happening to me. I'm a child, a virgin. Help me, somebody. Help me!" This is all that I could scream but not on the outside. My mother never would have believe this. No way would I ever be able to tell this to anybody. This girl had set me and my family up to be able to control our whole house. My mother thought the world of her. So did my oldest brother. In their eyes she could do no wrong. My biological brother had been through enough over the years and he just wanted to play football, eat and have fun. No need in tearing him down any more. So, I had to touch her whenever she told me to.

God knew what was going on and he set a plan in motion to expose her another way. My mother began to get complaints from the men in the club and my brother about how she had set them on fire sexually. Again, I overheard it. I was so nosy because she kept me in the house. My mom finally faced up to what people were saying and sent her packing. Man, I was so glad when she left. You see, I could not tell anyone, but God knew and He's the One who got her out of our house. Ever since I received Christ in my life at the age of seven the Lord has continually protected me. He made a way out of no way. He's faithful to His word, I tell you. He'll never leave you nor forsake you. When your father and your mother forsake you then He will take you up.

By this time I was beginning to shut down against family. It did not matter who came. I wanted them to stay away from me. You know, it's a shame that a child cannot find protection in his own home. Many parents today cannot do anything right for their children or tell them what to. They don't know how to reach their kids. It could be that someone has touched that child and he has shut down for fear of telling the parent about it, or you have been protecting your own past touching and will not touch their bottom with a belt. Kids today get away with everything to the point that they go and shoot up a whole school or community because you told them no and you meant it for once. Let me pause here a moment. If half the kids today went through half of what I went through then I could almost understand them slipping over the edge a little. But many parents don't even hit their kids. They are afraid of the Department of Children and Family Services coming in and taking them to jail. This is the lie that America wants you to believe today, but the truth of the matter is that we, in America, let one ignorant woman take prayer out of school. Wake up America and let's start praying again at home and in school. Send their behinds to church at an early age like I went and when they come up against something they cannot handle they have a prayer partner that already knows about their troubles and He will keep them, I promise you. What does America have to lose? Let's go back to praying in school. Put it back. I know God will keep our children's minds in perfect peace because He kept my mind through everything I suffered because at the age of seven I asked God to come into my life. I was kept even though I got into many fights after school. Nobody got killed, and the next day or two we, as kids, were playing again and I was not on trial for murder. My parents did not have to move away because of shame. Come on America! Let's pray.

After my cousin left I went through the rest of that year in a calm state. My mother seemed to calm down more and more, thank you Jesus. My mother gave her life to the Lord by the time I was twelve years old and then things really quieted down in our house. No more men in the house. No parties. We had it going on. My mother would get dressed and look so pretty, just strutting her stuff up the street. She would walk to church sometimes instead of being picked up. My mother never drove. She look good and I could tell that she felt good by the way she held her head up. When she came home on Sunday afternoon, the men on the street would be smiling and trying to get their talk on with her, but she would just laugh and say, "You see my kids with me, don't you?" We would come home and she would heat up the food and tell us about church, about how they just praised the Lord. She said everybody around her was just a running and shouting. She said it felt good. I got goose bumps just listening to her. I felt so warm inside as she talked. Boy, she could really be nice if she just stayed in church. I had never seen her so happy, and I was so proud of my mother when she got dressed up. Man, she was beautiful. I wanted to hug her and tell her that I loved her, but that kind of talk was not done around our house, and I was afraid she would hit me or push me away. I could not take any more pain and I did not want to upset her. Not now. "Let's just leave well enough alone," I thought.

By this time I was going to afternoon therapy classes to see what made me act out the way I did. How could you just put a child in therapy and not the parent? That should be a given any time a child tells you she never gets to go outside and play with kids her own age. I was always around grownups. This should be a red flag for any teacher, principal or therapist. You would not need a college degree to see that, maybe, we need to look into why this child is not allowed to play. Is the child being held prisoner in her own home? Is she being abused or molested? These are questions that should be raised in that type of situation. Why isn't a child being allowed to play? I could go out to play in the snow with my brother in the back yard, but when he had other plans I had to stay upstairs and talk to the other kids in the yard from the balcony. But God allowed me to endure it all.

My mother continued to go to church. We did not have much money coming in because there were no more parties. But who cared? We all pitched in and did what we had to do. My mother stopped playing the lottery as well. Everyday the adults would play what they called "street numbers" and if you hit you got money for that chosen number being picked that day. That was something like the lotto is now, but it was run by the mob. My mother would play everyday hoping to hit so that we would have money. She would get a number from this idiot in New York, like he really knew a winning number. If he really knew what numbers to play don't you think he would hit it himself. Please! My mother believed in some weird stuff, but when you are raised that way you see it as being right. Well, I never saw that man but I knew deep down inside he was a fake, a phony taking people's money.

One day my mother told me he had died. His wife said they had eaten Sunday dinner and she went up to bed for the night. It was early, so he said he would stay down stairs a while and close up the house before coming up. He wanted to read the newspaper. She said she woke up about three in the morning and he was not in the bed, so she went downstairs to check on her husband and found him dead, sitting up in the chair. I laughed out loud and said, "Did he know if he was going to die?" My mother looked at me. I quickly said, "I'm not laughing at the man dying; I'm laughing at whether he knew he was going to die? He can tell you who put roots on you and give you this stuff to drink to make you feel better and tell you your belly is swollen because you've got a snake wrapped up in you, then how come he didn't know he was going to die? Did he blame it on the cabbage boy?" I laughed. I'll never forget that because it came up from out of nowhere. My mother looked at me and then she said, "Don't worry about what he knew. You just worry about getting that kitchen clean.

Like I said, my mother had begun to change right before my own eyes. She was being delivered and I could see her new life forming, praise the good Lord. I'm not here to preach but just to share my life story. As for me, life slowed down only inside the house. My inner man was still a wreck, as I shared earlier. I had left church but I believed God lived in heaven and I should pray to Him every single day, which I did. I had no other knowledge of Him from Bible reading or teaching. I did something I should not have done only because I had picked up the lust demon all these other people had on them. I ask God, again, to forgive me for my wrongdoing, in the name of Jesus. Lord, I'm sorry. Forgive me for the part I played in these sexual issues, in Jesus' name. I repent publicly in this book. I am so sorry for my wrong.

Now don't go thinking that I slept with some women. The devil is a liar and so are you if that's what entered your mind at this point. You see, even though I touched my cousin, I did that because she made me. I may not have had the brains she had, but I knew deep down inside of me that God did not make me to lay with a women as if she or I was a man. No way did I ever think that. It was engraved in my heart that that was wrong. God is the creator of everything in heaven, on earth and under the earth, and I'm not going to tell you that I would lay with a woman and then blame the all-knowing God. I don't think so. God forgive all you other lying wonders who are saying and believing it. God did not make you a man trapped in a woman's body or a woman trapped in a man's body. The devil has you trapped in emotional trauma. The homosexual lifestyle exposed you to the familiar spirits that were on that person of the same sex. You hooked up with them for companionship, identifying that you both had been hurt severely in the past. God had nothing to do with that mess. It was the devil and he told you to blame God.

I used to baby sit for three lesbian women. They had a lot of the same issues. They were all shorter than five feet tall and they all came from broken homes, abandon by one of the parents, if not both. None of them liked school. They all lived in the same neighborhood, went to same school, dressed very well and had one or no other siblings. They also had boyfriends, but the boyfriends cheated and beat on them. In spite of this they had children by these boys and were forced to get married so their families would not be shamed. I saw these beautiful girls grow up to be lesbians. When I babysat for them I would see them go out at night dressed like men, looking like the boyfriend or the husband. Man, that confused me. I asked them why they lived like this and one told me, "When you get older and a man is putting his fist upside this head right here (pointing to my head) and you have not done anything at all to him and you tell him to stop and then after beating you and kicking you he wants you to take off all the clothes he did not already tear off, then you tell me what use you would have for one man. I don't ever want to smell another man's sweat next to me. Now, if he's just sleeping with me, that's something different." I share this so you can see that trauma made them choose that lifestyle. They never blamed God. They just said that you never know what hand life is going to deal you; just be the best player that you can be. Trust me, my life did not start out easy. But to sleep with a woman? No way. Wow! I had an urgency to share that with whoever reads this book.

Being thirteen I was just starting to form my own thoughts, doing my own thing. I went out with my brothers on recreation night until eight o'clock if all my chores were done. I tried to stay on top of them because I did not want any trouble from my mom. Then one day I came in from school to see my mother looking like she had lost her way again. She was not drunk but was clearly upset, yelling at her "king", my older brother. She was so upset with him that she stuck him several times with her fist. That scared me. She never raised her hand to hit him, not in a hurtful way. Now she was going at it with him. I waited and just listened to find out what was going on. She kept yelling, "Ho, where are we going to do this? What made you be so stupid? You both should have come to me. Now what do we do? I cannot make this go away. This woman wanted to lock you up. If it was not for the girl she would have. I do not have room for her and her baby." Ok, now I got it. My brother had gone out and knocked up this fifteen year old girl. He was seventeen. She and her sister had lied to him about her age, but nevertheless, he was in hot water with her mother. My mother was upset because the girl's mother had thrown her and the baby out of her house with nowhere to live. She had two older sisters who lived at home, but they were not ready to leave home to help their baby sister. So we had to.

I said out of nowhere, "Mama, let her come here with the baby. We can make room for her in the girls' room. The baby can sleep with me and we'll put her on the couch." Well, it did not sit well with her, but she had no other choice. This was her granddaughter. Oh, what a beautiful baby. They moved in and I kept her baby while she went to night school to finish her education. My mother laid down the rules for the girl and my brother. Even if my brother wanted to bother her in my mother's house, she was so afraid of my mother that she would not disrespect our home. She and I became very close. To this day she is my older sister. I never had one but she became that for me. I love her and she has always loved me. I took very good care of my niece and helped out whenever I could. She was always there for me during my emotional struggles at home as a young teenager. She helped me get through tough times. She hurt a lot because of her mother's cold-plated heart. She sought love from my brother but did not get it. They fought all the time. She wanted to be with him, but he wanted to run the streets. They had this young child that needed her mother, who ran the streets as well. Eventually, her oldest sister got an apartment and the two of them moved in together, which was so nice because I started staying the weekends over there babysitting for my niece and the sister's son. This was fine by me. I could be there in peace with no one to bother me. However, that only lasted a hot minute. My mother, again, needed me at home.

By this time I'm at wit's end with "do this" and "do that". I started staying out later than I was suppose to. I started sneaking out when my mother went to bed. Now I was fourteen years old and did not listen to anyone. I didn't want to. I got a job from Monday to Friday after school. I gave my mother the money and went out on Friday nights to the teen dance at the teen center. She did not mind because she could look out the window when the dance was over and watch me and my brother walk home. I joined the dance contest one night at the teen center and I won first place. Boy, I loved to dance and I was good at it. I started dancing all over the city, competing against other couples. I would pick a partner, and once I started out with him I had to finish the competition with him. Believe it or not, for almost two years I won first place every time I danced. My partner and I were good. I didn't date boys; I just liked to party because I had a love for dancing.

One weekend the teen center traveled to Boston for a show down between the Connecticut and the Boston teen center. Boy, this was going to be big. My brother and all the neighbors kept saying during that week leading up to the trip, "We know who's going to bring home that trophy, don't we?" I would just smile. I had something that gave me joy, something that I didn't even have to work hard at. I would look at others dancing and the next thing I knew I could do that dance better than them. My mother said, "Who told you that you were going to Boston? I do not remember anyone saying a thing about you going to Boston or anywhere else, for that matter." I said, "Mama, I can win this contest. Please let me go. There's a hundred dollar prize as well as a trophy." After that she said that I could go but I realized it was all about the money. After each contest the winner would get money. I would just give it to her and parade around knowing that I had won. You know, I looked at my mother that day we were leaving and she kept smiling as everyone told me to bring back the trophy and make them proud. They told me to enjoy myself. Neighbors were saying the very things I wanted my mother to say, but she only said to me, "Behave yourself and bring back that money." I guess that was her way of saying "Win, girl I know you can", because how else would I bring back the money unless I won it.

Boston was fun. Man, I felt grown being away from my mother by myself. My brother went but he was with his friends, and the rule was I did nothing and I didn't go anywhere without checking in with him. Otherwise, I had to stay with him and his buddies. I did as my brother told me and he was having the time of his life, as well. During the afternoon we had the pool area just for the teen centers that had traveled to Boston, along with the Boston teens. I got into a pink two-piece bathing suit. Boy, I tell you, I was shapely at that age. I went to take a picture on the diving board and, as I was getting my pose just right, this white boy came running up on the diving board and tossed me right in the water with him. It was eight feet of water and I did not know how to swim. As I was going down I saw my brother coming through the door. As I'm yelling that I can't swim, my brother dives in right as I hit the water. I saw all that water and I just knew I was dead. My brother was a great swimmer. He always jumped off the rocks at the beach and swam there. My mother could not afford swimming lessons, so he taught himself. I was glad to feel my brother's arms around my waist. He had saved his sister's life. Praise the Lord! I was scared but glad to be alive. After that I did not care about the dance contest or anything else. I was alive and that was all that mattered.

The contest was that night. I was too sick to think about dancing, but I did not want to let my brother down. I danced but I lost. Boston was hot. I could not even get close to dancing as good as the Boston girls. I did not feel bad because I lost. I was still the best ever, but I just didn't do well that night and it was fine by me. Who cared about winning when I had a great brother who believed in me? He said, "Sis, you are the best. You know that don't you?" He winked at me and said, "I love you even if you never win another contest. You are a great dancer. Don't worry about what nobody else says, you are good and that's all that matters to me. I'm proud of you." Wow! That meant the world to me to have my brother lift me up and encourage me like that because I could take that with me wherever I went. I knew that he loved me no matter what I could or could not do. I learned that day, that it is not always about winning but about staying in the game. That makes you a winner, as well. The race is not given to the swift but to those that endure to the end.

After I failed to win the contest, my brother and I began to seek out different friends and we didn't always like the friends that the other had chosen. He had to start working to help out at the house. My mother always did everything for my oldest brother, but not for my biological brother. It did not seem to bother him until he began to look at young girls in a different way. He wanted to dress better but he was too rough for the style of clothing my oldest brother wore. We both were now in high school. I was a freshman and he was a sophomore. He was light-skinned and very handsome, but my brother suffered from a learning disability and caught on to things a little slower than I did. My brother was great at fixing things. He could take things apart and put them back together again. Well, he started to hang around guys that he always had to prove himself to by doing dumb things like catching knives with his bare hands and getting cut. This hurt me because when he was hurt, then I was hurt. My brother got a job at night working at this factory. After a while, he began to hang out after work and would not come home. My mother found out that he was drinking and sleeping with a thirty-eight year old woman. Well, my mother went off. She said that this woman could not get a man but had to get a school kid to "rock her world". It took some time before we could convince him that she was too old for him. She ended up taking his money.

Then my brother found another girl. She seemed very nice, but she used him also. My mother wanted me to beat up the girl and I said, "I'm not bothering that girl for him. These are his choices, not mine to make for him. He needs to learn about this stuff for himself." This made her very mad and she tore into me like a mad woman saying, "Don't stand there in my house and tell me what you're not going to do." I told myself that when that beating was over she would never, ever, put her hands on me again. I was so angry with her I could have kicked her behind. I was fifteen and in high school and she was still beating on me? That was it. When she stopped hitting me with everything she had in her and everything she could find around her, I packed my stuff and I left. I just walked out. She tried to stab me, but I made it out the door. I do think she was really going to stab me, but I surely was not staying around to find out.

I went to a girlfriend's house. She and I happened to have the same name. Her mother said I had to wait until her husband came home to ask if I could spend the night. When he came home he said I could stay only for the night and after school I had to go home. He thought that my mother would have cooled down by then. I told myself that I didn't care never cooled off. I wasn't going back there. I was too old for her to keep putting scars on my body. My girlfriend's mother was very easygoing, so my friend kept sneaking me in after her father and mother went to sleep. Her mother knew every morning that I was there. She felt that she owed me because I stopped the neighborhood kids from beating up her daughter every other day. I never believed in you beating on someone that was no competition for you. Fight somebody who's going to give you a fight back. Don't just beat on a person that you know is not going to fight back. That's just being a bully and I hated bullies. I would walk up on a fight and see a helpless person getting beat down and I would jump in and fight for them. I did not have to know the person. It's just not right for anybody to beat on anyone who cannot defend themselves.

One night my friend and I went to the house of a boy we knew. My friend liked one of the boys and he had a good looking friend. His mother ran a very loose house and I mean "loose". Sometimes she did not even know who was in her house. Her husband was never in the house but was always sitting outside in the parking lot with his men friends, drinking until he was ready to go to bed. Well, I started to date this boy. By now I had been away from home for about three weeks, but I still went to school everyday. My friend's mother ran into my mother at the store and she threatened to have her put in jail because I was still a minor. So, I went back home, but now I'm dating this guy and my mother is telling me that I can't go out. Boy, I was getting red hot on the inside. I needed someone to understand me, but there just wasn't anybody around that I could talk to. My head began to hurt and I knew I had to talk to my boyfriend. He was a senior at a different high school so only my friend knew him. She swore on a stack of bibles not to tell if I got caught sneaking out. We ended up meeting two blocks from my house and I didn't get caught. He said all the right things to a freshman high school girl. I was in love.

We agreed to meet that weekend at his house to talk some more. I could not wait to see him. It made my week go by that much smoother. When the weekend came it seemed like my mother had so much work for me to do. I did everything she asked, and, when night came, I got the little ones in the tub and in front of the TV. After that, I was out the door. I had lied and told my mother I was going to a dance. When I left the house I was all dressed up and my mother had no idea what I was really planning to do. I went to my boyfriend's house with my girlfriend, who also sneaked out with me because she liked the other guy. We had some drinks and some more drinks. After a while I was drunk and you already know what happened. That senior took advantage of me. I told him no, and no was supposed to mean no. My mother's rule had always stayed in my mind. She would say, "You put your clothes on in this house and this is where they come off, and I mean just what I say. Not a stitch of clothes will I ever hear of you taking off outside of this house or you will regret the day you were born." This guy had sex with me and I did not say yes. I do not even remember feeling him. What a waste of time, I thought.

A few months later I missed my period. Can you imagine me telling my mother that? I know you can't because I couldn't either. Well, I ran to my niece's mother and told her what had happened. She yelled at me for not coming to her earlier and told her older sister who said that I needed to tell my mother right away. I asked my niece's mother to tell her, but everybody was afraid of my mother. She was mean to me, but very nice to everybody else, so nobody wanted to get on her bad side. I told my niece's mother, who was like my big sister, and she said she would talk to my mother. She told me not to expect anything good to come from it. She said I should have known better, especially since my mother treated me different from the other kids. Then she told me, "Besides, I'm not going to feel sorry for you. Look at what I went through with your brother. He never looked back after he got what he wanted from me, and now I've got this child here to take care of. You knew better than to put yourself in that kind of situation." She agreed to talk to my mother, but I was scared because she did not say when she would talk to her, just that she would.

A few days later I came in from school and trouble was waiting for me at the door. My mother met me at the door and told me to go to the doctor with my niece's mother. She did not look at me. I asked, "When?" and she said, "You better be on your way down them stairs now." So I took off down the street to my niece's mother's house. When I got there she told me that I had hurt my mother real bad. I told her that I had not planned for this to happen and that I had gotten drunk. She went off on me for the first time ever. She yelled at me and cried, telling me that I put my future in danger as well as my life. She told me that I was too young to have a baby and too smart for this type of life.

She said that I was a teenager, not an adult, and that I'm not supposed to go around talking about getting drunk and switching my behind. "You still have a lot of growing up to do," she said, "and your mother wants you to have a better life. And what do you do? You get drunk like you are an adult and come back home with a belly full. I want you to stop this mess now before you really get yourself in trouble, you hear me? Stop it now. No more of this stupid talk about getting drunk or even drinking period, you hear me?" I looked at her and I said, "Yes, I hear you."

A very interesting thing happened that day. When she spoke to me I felt that she really cared for me. Just as I was thinking it she said, "I know I'm hard on you today and I don't want to be because you don't need anybody else in your life being hard on you. You've suffered enough harsh treatment already. I love and I want you to get your education and make a better life for yourself. Your whole life is ahead of you and you will not come around me drunk or talk that way again about getting drunk. That's not cute. You are a very pretty girl. Women would die for the shape you've got. Men will promise a young girl like you the world just to be in your company. Do something with your life from this point on or do not come back around me. I love you and I will not watch you go down hill. You are too smart for this type of behavior." She took me to the doctor and all the way there on the bus thoughts of the talk ran through my head. She really loved me. I had a real big sister who loved me.

The doctor examined me and told me that, yes, I was pregnant. He never said when my baby was due, just to have my mother call him. My niece's mother asked what I thought my mother was going to say. I said, "The damage is done now. What can she say?" I looked at her and I started to cry, something I had not done very much only because I had become numb to pain. For some reason that question made me cry. What would a mother do to a daughter she never really wanted anyway? What could she say that would make my life better or worse off? Well, when we got back home my niece's mother told her what the doctor said and she left, but not before my mother said, "You see why I don't let her out?" My mother rolled her eyes at me and did not say a word to me. She picked up the telephone and asked the neighbor across the street to come over to talk. This neighbor had been a friend to me as well. She came over and spoke to me and said that I should have told her even if I was afraid to tell my mother. "I would have helped," she said. "He raped you and you did not say nothing to nobody." I just looked at her. My mother had told her my private business. After that my mother told her to come to the front of the house so they could talk about something else in private. As the neighbor was about to leave she asked me if I wanted some ice cream or something. I told her I wasn't hungry, but she kept trying to get me to go with her to get ice cream. I finally told her that I wasn't allowed to leave the house, not even to go on the back porch. She look at my mother, who then said, "I don't care where she goes. She didn't ask me to leave when she got her belly full. Why ask to go now?" I did not know what to do so I just left.

We walked to the ice cream parlor and then to the park. We just walked and talked about nothing, really. We finally ended up back home and the neighbor spoke briefly to my mother before she left and went home. The next morning was a Saturday morning. My mother was in the kitchen and I had slept late. I'm in trouble now, I thought. I ran into the bathroom and heard her yell, "Get you a bath while you are in there." I thought it was too early to take a bath, but she said that I might not have time later to take one. I went ahead and took one, thinking she had an errand for me to run. When I got out of the tub and got dressed I went into the kitchen only to find our neighbor there. She came over early on Saturday morning when her man stayed out all night. She and my mother had coffee and talked. My mother was like an aunt to her and she loved my mother. I thought she was crazy. Nobody should have liked my mother, I thought. She would give you the clothes off her back, feed you and share with you. She just did not like me.

After I arrived in the kitchen, I said good morning to everyone and I headed to the refrigerator to get the milk to eat cereal. My mother told me to put the milk down, put on my shoes and go with our neighbor. I did as I was told and left with the neighbor. After we walked about a block I asked where we were going. She said, "Your mother asked me to take you to see this Spanish lady friend of mine. She's real good. She will not hurt you or nothing. I've used her several times myself." Stupid me, I kept walking, not knowing what the heck this lady was really talking about. We finally arrived at the Spanish lady's house. When we walked in the house, the two of them spoke for a couple of minutes on the other side of a draped room. I could see their feet but could not hear what they were saying. My heart started to beat when they opened up the curtain and called me in. The lady did not say a word. She motioned for me to take off my panties. I just looked at her. My neighbor said, "Girl, you better listen to that women. You do not want your mother to bring you down here." So, I did what she told me to do and I lay down. She propped my legs up, squirted some cold stuff up in me and told me to get up. That was it. I looked at my neighbor and, my God, my life died right in that cold dark room. I walked home with her in silence, not saying a word. There was nothing to be said. My mother had paid this Spanish lady to kill my unborn child and she could have killed me as well. The neighbor said, "I know you may not understand this now and you may be upset with me and your mama, but it is for your own good. You are too young to bring a child into this world with no help. I would not have done this if your mother had not made me promise last night to take you. Please don't be mad with me. I love you." But what did I need anybody's love for? All anyone that was supposed to love me ever did was hurt me, damage me, and leave me alone. I was quiet all the way back to the house. How do I live with this woman? How do I take her? What now, world? What do I do now? These questions raced through my mind. I was losing it fast. "God help me, Lord help me, please help me," I kept thinking to myself.

My mother got the report of what happened when we got back to the house. She still had not spoken to me in days, but yet she is slowly killing me off. I went to lay down. The whole ordeal made me sick. I stayed in bed all day until about three in the afternoon and my stomach began to cramp like crazy. I was having a hard time so I called my mother to help me. She sent my sister to check on me and my sister said, "Mom, you better come in here. There is blood on her clothes. She called the doctor and then she came in and asked me how long I had been having pains, and I told her that I woke up with them. She got up and said that it would all be over in a few minutes and walked off. She called her neighbor friend over again and she sat with me. Finally, at about four o'clock in the evening they took me and a fetus, a little boy, to Bridgeport hospital. My family doctor was aware of this home abortion and so was the hospital. I smelled like Pine-sol and some type of hair gel. The hair gel was to keep the Pine-sol from burning my insides. The doctor knew something but my mother would not leave the room for them to talk to me. They tried several times but she stayed right in the room with me. I didn't matter. I couldn't have talked anyway. Emotionally, I was gone for good.

I came home and stayed out of school for two days. I went to my niece's mother's house and told her what my mother had done. She already knew. She cried and I asked her why she was crying. "It wasn't you or your baby," I said. I went on to say, "I never had a chance to make any decision about the baby or anything. Just squeeze and out it comes. Now, life goes on." She told me that sometimes life deals you a bad hand, but that does not mean that you stay there. She said I had to get myself up and start over again. Only this time I had to think before I found myself around bad people. "Everybody is not going to help you and everybody is not going to hurt you," she said. "Find those you need to be with, but better yet, be by yourself. You don't need friends. They are trouble. Get to yourself and do for yourself. Don't look to them to help you, but help them instead." My niece's mom did not make sense to a lot of people, but I knew what she meant. Stop depending on others to make your life different or better. Make it that way for yourself, then help them by being a good example. That's what she was saying to me.

I started doing just that. I excelled in school. I made good grades and took a lot of after school and weekend classes so that I could get enough credits to go to college. I could make it into college. I even did the Upward Bound program on weekends instead of running the streets. I was gaining so much out of these classes and activities that my friends became jealous of me. That was ok, though. They still needed me to help them make it out of high school. By the time I entered my junior year in high school, I had enough credits to graduate a year early. However, I wanted to come out with my girls so I stayed through my senior year, only going to school two hours a day for English and gym. I became Vice-President of my junior class as well as queen of my junior ring dance. I was doing great. I did not go out and party. I would just go to my niece's house and hang around there. I would babysit for my niece's mom so she could get a break. I loved my niece and I always made sure she had nice clothes. I worked at McDonald's after school from the tenth grade until I graduated. I put myself through school, staying at home and paying my way, not really having much to say to anyone after the abortion ordeal.

After a school dance one night my girlfriend and her boyfriend rode by my niece's mom's house. We were all sitting on the front porch and she had the driver stop. It was a friend of my oldest brother who was home from the Vietnam War for the weekend. He was tall and quite spirited. She was trying to fix me up with a date, but I just was not interested. Out of respect, I met him and said hello. We chatted a bit and I asked him when he was getting out. He said that he had thirty more days and then he would be home for good. He told me that I had grown up to be a very attractive lady. I thanked him for the compliment and wished him well. Then, out of nowhere, I said, "Thanks for fighting to keep us safe." He called me to the car asked if he could hug me for that comment. I let him hug me and then he drove off. After going only a few feet, the car stopped and backed up. He leaned out and asked if he could write me and I told him he could. I did not give him another thought. He was too old for me, and after that first go around I was done. Later, my oldest brother asked if I would go to the prom with his friend's brother. I said, "No, thank you." He then admitted to me that the guy could not get a date if you paid for him. No girl wanted to go out with him, let alone to the prom. I had seen this guy at school. He looked good, but that was my own opinion not someone else's. I felt sorry for him, so I went out with him. After being in the car with him for twenty minutes this guy's breath was dead. It stank really bad. I put the window down and hoped that he wouldn't say anything. I did tell him after we took the picture to not come near me again until it was time to go home and he agreed. I told him he was a nice looking guy but he just needed to pay more attention to his breath. That's what was keeping the girls away from him. I did not do it in a manner that would hurt him, but I did make sure he got the point where he would not be caught out like that again.

The guy from the army and I crossed paths again about six months later. We met at a club. After he took me out to eat, we drove around and talked for hours. We stayed up all night in his red Volkswagen. It was day break and I had him drop me off at my niece's house and I walked home from there just to keep the peace. Something felt good about him. We spent a lot of time together. We laughed a lot about life and other people, and he shared a lot about the war. It was my senior year and I did not want to go to my prom. He was too old anyway. So, I pretended to want to go but instead I went with him and my girls to a club in New Haven. They all seemed a little too laid back for me. Then I kept watching them and saw that they were all sniffing white stuff up their nose. I asked my girl what she was doing. She offered me some and he snatched her hands back. He said, "This is my lady. If I want her to have this I'll give it to her, ok?" My girl told him to chill and stop being so uptight. "She's green. She doesn't go anywhere and does not know about this," she said about me. He said, "That's the whole point. Let's leave it that way." He seemed upset, so I said, "Let's just all get along. Is that alright?"

We began dating that night. Before, we were just spending time out together clubbing, nothing serious. Later that week I learned that he was a small time drug dealer from out of 'Nam (that's what they called it back then). I felt big after learning that about him. I pretended not to know and waited for him to tell me. See, I had asked my friend about the white powder situation and she said, "He is a drug dealer and we all were sniffing heroin and he did not want you in on it. I didn't know he had not told you so that's why I offered some to you." This is how I found out about it, but I wanted him to tell me himself. They stayed up late every night, but I had to go to school. So he would drop me off at home and their little party kept on until daybreak. One weekend I got upset with him because all these girls from the other side of town started looking for him. They were knocking on his door and the back and forth traffic was getting larger by the hour. I told him I needed to leave. His life was just a little too busy for me. He then said he had something to tell me and asked if he could pick me up later that evening. I told him to call me first. He came to my home, instead, and introduced himself to my mother. He asked her if he could see me and take me out. I heard her laughing on the back porch as she was calling me outside. I looked out to see him and, man, I got scared. She said, "This man wants to know if it is ok if he takes you out. I told him that would have to be your own choice, not mine." I looked at him as if to say, "Man, you are trying to get me killed?"

We left my house and he told me he wanted to start all over with me as his real girl. I told him he had to do everything the proper way. That was when he shared with me about the drug dealing. He just wanted a little quick money to get on his feet after coming home from the war. He said that the government did not give him much to start over with. I asked him how he planned on selling drugs and not going to jail. He said, "Baby, I won't be in it that long." Oh, how wrong that statement proved to be for the both of us. I wanted to be with him more then because of how he handled himself in the streets and with my mother. He respected her very much but he did not let her talk to me any way she wanted to. He stood up to her but was never rude. He just spoke his peace and moved on. I would feel distant from him only when they had their little drug gatherings and I did not want to be left out. So, I fussed with him about it and asked him to let me sniff a little, too. He said he didn't want that for me. He wanted me to finish high school and get into college. My God, this man sounded like my mother. This only made me mad, which made me want to do it more. He said it because he loved me, but I couldn't see that. All I heard was my mama when he said those words to me. I thought he was doing this because of her.

We fussed for days, but I finally left him alone about it. I called myself outsmarting him. I did not know about the dark world of addiction. But he did, and he loved me enough to try to keep me from it. But because I so desperately wanted to be a part of his life, to be fully connected to him, I had to be involved in everything he did. So I would sneak a few blows behind his back from my girl or from one of his boys that was sniffing in the room or car. I would do it when he was not looking or when he went to answer the door. I could not keep that up for long because I threw up right after I took a hit. It began to drip down my nasal passage. He told me one night, "Girl, you better make sure you're taking them birth control pills. Your mother is not going to cut my jewelry off because you're not doing what you're suppose to." I laughed because I knew better than to go home knocked up again. I had not forgotten what she had done.

I got used to feeling numb all the time so that nothing mattered to me but him. He did everything for me. He bought my clothes, kept money in my pocket at all times, and made sure I had lunch and the very best outfits. The boosters (shoplifters) used to come by every day with clothes my size and he would by almost everything they brought him. He would trade a bag of blow for an outfit. These girls were good boosters. They would sell out and go back to the same store and get some more stuff to trade for drugs. Of course, they got money too. They had kids to support, but that high came first. I said to one of them that I would never do that. I could not see myself ever living that way. And to beg? Please! That was the pits right there. I'm too smart to get caught like that. **I did not know what I was saying about the disease world I had just stepped into voluntary**. I finally graduated and, man, did I cry. He looked at me and said, "Well baby, you made it. He was so proud of me and asked if I heard him yell for me. I had gotten a four-year scholarship to college in Boston. I was the first black female at our school to get a full four-year scholarship. I only had to pay for my books. My mother was at my graduation. She only wanted that stupid diploma. I gave it to her and I walked away. Yes, you could look at her and tell she was so happy, but look what she put me through to get there. She said, "I knew you could do it. You were nobody's dummy. I just had to make sure you went all the way and finished like I did not do. Because I never got mine I wanted to make sure you get yours." This was all she wanted and she put me through all that misery for that. Well, I left home that night for good and moved in with my boyfriend. He continued to make sure she saw me every day, and if she or my little sisters needed anything he made sure they got it. He gave my mother money as well. She knew about him selling drugs, but it did not seem to bother her that I was going out with a drug dealer. She did tell me to watch myself and to be careful because "those people are crazy."

I learned a lot that summer. I learned to count drugs in bundles, cut drugs and bag drugs. My habit increased to the point where I did not care if he knew I was getting high. As a matter of a fact, he gave me my first bag of pure heroin on graduation night. He said, "You are done now with people making decisions for you. Now learn to make them for yourself. I'm going to teach you how to make money. Don't let money make you. The love of money is the root of all evil." I was on my way. I now had power and control. I had what others needed and plenty of it. We sold drugs night and day, twenty-four-seven, 365 days a year. We had to shut down one week just to spend time together. We sniffed all day long. Soon it was time for me to leave for college. I had been with this man everyday since I was seventeen years old and you did not see him without me. So, it was hard to go. I did not want to leave him. He promised to ride up to Boston to see me every chance he got. I would be tired of him, he told me. That's how much he would be there.

I went home because my mother had sent my brother to remind me to come by the house to see my sisters and brothers before I left. She wanted to see me before I left, too. I know that was the real deal. It hurt that she could never tell me she loved me and was proud of me. I bust my butt the last three years of high school so she could be proud of me and all she could say was, "I knew you had it in you. I just had to make sure you did it." I loved my mother. It was just sad how we communicated with each other. I never disrespected her in her own house nor would I ever do that. When I left for college all the neighbors were out on the porch to say their good byes. I reached over to kiss my mother and she turned her cheek to me as if she did not really want me to put my lips on her. Before I left I told her I would call as soon as I got there. My boyfriend had a surprise for me. He and his friend drove me all the way to school. That help me a lot, but I wish now that I had taken the bus. Maybe time alone would have helped me to focus more on my future. Riding the bus up to Boston could have help my mind to settle down.

We headed for Boston. I felt good about being with my boyfriend. Having my man take me to school was great. We got high on the way up there and when we arrived he gave me three bags of pure heroine to take me through the weekend. Then he said, "Baby, you need to get your mind on school and only school. I'll be back to see you this weekend, ok?" We pulled up in front of my dorm, and when he unloaded my things I started tripping. I was like, "What are you doing? Don't leave me here." He told me to get my butt in my room. This was going to be my life for the next four years. "I'm so proud of you," he said, "and I love you. Do this for us, ok?" I started crying. I thought the best days of my life were coming to a close. He cried, too. He asked me not to put him through this. It was hard for both of us because we been together everyday. He told me we were still going to be together but that I had to do this for us. He kept telling me not to cry and to hold my head up. I heard everything but I could not focus on it. I broke away and went upstairs to put my things away and sign in. He left and I just fell across the bed crying to myself.

I heard my name being called to come bring my things upstairs. That's when I remembered I had forgot my clothes at the bottom of the stairs. Men were not allowed in the female dorm area at all so I had to drag them upstairs myself. There was a house meeting where we would be introduced to the house mom, her husband and the rest of the girls in the dorm. I was stone out of my mind. That blow was stronger than I thought, so I kept nodding out. This girl next to me kept elbowing me to wake up and I was glad she had my back. The house mom could tell that many of us were tired and were ready to go to bed. She told us we would pick back up again the next night around 7:30. I thanked the girl for having my back and I took off upstairs. Once I got in my room I laid down just to enjoy my high and not be on the floor. The next day I got my books, signed in for classes and then walked around the campus to see where I really was. I kept my drugs on me at all times, going in and out of the rest room to sniff a little. After my fourth day at school I was out of drugs. It was now time to focus on class work and studies. I was ready to begin my life as a college student.

Two days with no drugs and my eyes started to water a lot. I kept yawning like I needed sleep. I could not understand it but I noticed a change in my body happening rapidly. By the fifth day I was cold and my nose kept running. By the sixth day I started getting these headaches that felt like a car was in my head. Then the runs came. On the ninth day, I was sitting in class and the teacher started to lecture. He talked for what seemed like hours. All of a sudden, I closed my book. **I got this rush from my pass** and I stood up. The teacher stopped and asked me where I was going. I said to him, "I am sick and tired of people telling me what to do. 'Carolyn turn to page,' 'Carolyn do this,' Carolyn do that.'" Everyone was looking at me. I said, "Sir, give this scholarship to someone that is ready for it. I'm too tired to turn another page right now," and walked out. I was going through withdrawal from pure heroine and did not know it. I just needed to get out of there fast so I could think. The house mom was at the door when I arrived back at the dorm. She tried to talk to me, but I was to sick to listen. I had been gone too long to stand still and I had been running for my life all my life. I could not stand still. I had hid everything behind the walls of getting high and everything seemed to come crashing back - my mom's voice in my head, the men's hands on my little bottom, my cousin forcing me to touch her. I needed to get out of there before I lost my mind, which seemed like it was already happening.

I had learned to survive on pills and then heroine. My life was a mess for real now. I needed to get to my man right then and nobody was going to stop me. I told the house mother she would never understand or believe me. Even if I wanted to tell her, where would I start? I asked her to call me a cab, but she said she would have to call my parents. I told her to do so because I didn't want something to happen to me and my mother sue the school. I went upstairs and packed my things. When I came downstairs she said my mother forbid her to call me a cab and I had to get home the best way I could. She said, "Carolyn, I'm sorry, but I have to listen to your mom." I asked if I could leave my suitcases until the next weekend and she said her husband would put them in a safe place. She said, "Carolyn, many young ladies leave home for the first time and are a little uncomfortable, but with our help they overcome it, some a little slower than others. They all do well here." I looked at her and I said, "Ma this has nothing to do with being away from home. I never really had one. There is not enough time in the day to tell you about me." You see, I did not know me either. I was a people pleaser and a drug abuser at the age of nineteen.

I left the dorm walking, barely able to remember how to get to the bus terminal. My mind was so fuzzy I could not remember everything she told me, so I walked until I stopped to ask for more directions and discovered I was not that close. If I had known I was that far from the bus terminal I would have called for my man to pick me up, but I wanted to surprise him. I finally made it to the bus terminal, paid for my ticket to get home, and waited for the bus to come. I was cold. Boston is a cold city anyway, but its September and I was freezing. Although I didn't know it at the time, I was experiencing one of my withdrawal symptoms.

The bus arrived on schedule and it took what seemed like a lifetime to get back to Connecticut. I knew my mother was going to be very upset with me, but I was sick and fed up. There was no need in anyone trying to make me go back to school. To make sure that would be the case I had told the school that I was turning down the scholarship and that I was not ready to continue my education at this time. When I arrived in Bridgeport I took a cab to my man's house. He was not at home but at the bar up the street. He had already heard from my mother that I had left school. He tried to talk me into staying with him for the weekend and then letting him take me back that Monday morning for class. I told him no and he began to yell at me. This man wanted a better life for me more than I did for myself. I just wanted to be with him. I was sick and I began to tell him about how bad I was feeling. He looked at me and said, "Girl, you done messed around and got yourself a drug habit. How could that have happened? I gave you the best." He did not know until then that I had been getting high behind his back with my girlfriend and one of his friends.

Well, I believe his world fell apart that night. He looked at me and he began to curse and cry. I mean, real tears. He told me that I was so pretty and I never needed to add anything to make a man accept me. "What man wouldn't want to be with you?" he asked. "You light up any room with your laughter and that smile. Why would you want to do such a thing to yourself?" I told him I did not feel a part of his life because I was always the one left out of the real party. He held me and we both cried. I told him I never felt a part of anyone. He said, "That's crazy. This is all so crazy. Carolyn, what is wrong? What is going on in that head of yours? What happened to you? I don't believe I really know who I fell in love with." I told him that if I had those answers I probably would have stayed at school. My life was what it was - shallow, dark, empty. I never really liked doing the things that I did but I did them to hold on until the next day came around. I told him that we had been together every single day but he had been too high to notice that I was always high. That week was the first time I had not been high in a long time. I didn't like to feel; I just wanted to laugh. He looked at me and said, "Girlfriend, this is your last day of that. I'm going to get you back to the real world if it is the last thing I do. We are going to leave these drugs alone together." He started doing drugs in the army to get the killing out of his mind. He couldn't get to sleep if he didn't sniff day in and day out. "But now," he said, "we both are done with it." Then I said, "In the meantime I need to be able to eat and hold it down." He told me I was out there, and then he opened a bag and we sniffed it together. In a few minutes I was alright again. My headache and all had gone away. I had to go home and deal with my mom, but now it was going to be a little bit easier. Whatever my mother said I could handle it.

Upon arriving at my mother's house I found her in the kitchen. I open the screen door in the back and she looked at me and said, "You finally made your way here after being in town all night?" I could not tell her that I had been too sick to come. I had a bad headache and I did not want to say things to her that I did not mean. Let me be clear about something. I have never, ever gotten so high that I used a curse word toward my mother. I loved her in spite of how sick our relationship was. She was my mother and I was told by many people to respect her even though she was hard on me. I would have better days ahead, they told me. I obeyed those old people and I gave her the utmost respect to her face. Now, when I was out of her hearing range, that was between the air and me what I said. Anyway, she told me to never put my feet back in her house and to go back to where I was last night. Since she could no longer tell me what to do, she told me not to come back unless I planned on going to college. I left the house knowing that I could not handle school at that time but hopeful to return some day.

My man and I started working on me not using drugs, but this only lasted a week because I caught him sniffing on the back porch early one morning. At the time I did not see the danger that lie in the darkness of this world of addiction, but I soon began to see it. I started traveling to New York to pick up drugs with him. I learned how to do this so that when he was selling good on the streets I could ride down to pick up and he would not have to be out long before I got back. I stayed high every day and was out late every night. Then I got pregnant with our first baby. He had a daughter already, but he could not get along with her mother. She was ok. A little homely looking, but ok. She worked a good job but she was just **too Green (Square in other words)**.

I continued to do drugs, but when he found out he punched me so hard in my face. I said, "Man, I got to get out of here. You are crazy." He told me that if he caught me doing drugs again with his baby girl he would kill me. Then he tore up the room. He had a temper with other people, but this was the first time with me. In fact, it was the first time I had been struck by any man, period. I left him when I was three months pregnant and went to stay with my girlfriend. I got money for doctor bills and for food, but I had nothing to do with him. But that only lasted a little while. I went back to him about a month later.

We went to New York to cop some drugs and head back to Connecticut. We had to go up these stairs, but I had to stop and rest because there were too many flights of stairs. He wished he had left me downstairs, but now we just had to keep going. Just as we stopped on the third landing two dudes who were hiding in the dark parts of the hallway came. One had a gun. He stuck it to my head and told my baby's father to give up the drugs and the money. He said, "Man don't hurt my woman. She's having a baby. I'll give you what you ask for." He reached into his pockets, gave up his money and turned his pockets out. They asked if that was all he had, and he told them he was only getting a little something for himself, not for me too. They let us go. Boy, that scared me. You see, we already knew about the stick-ups that had started going down in New York against Connecticut people. We were prepared in case we got stuck-up. We hid our main stash in my maternity clothes. However, I still did not want a gun pointed at me.

When we came back to Bridgeport I was not allowed to go back to New York until after I had the baby. That was not the end of the situation with the guys pulling the gun on me. My man had now become my baby's father. He could not let it rest about the gun ordeal. Every time he went down there he wanted to get them back and hoped that he and his boys would run into them. Well, one day it happened. They were in another hallway and the same thing happened again, but he recognized the guy's voice from the last time and, with his Vietnam self, he went after those guys. They beat them and some of the guys from the city beat them. They got tore up bad.

I finally had a six pound baby girl. My labor was very long and hard. I wished my mother would have come to sit with me, but she only visited one time. I had a midwife sit with me to help me push. After bringing the baby home I still used drugs and sold them from the house. My baby's father was handling someone else's product now and he had to pay upfront. Sometimes we did not have it, so all we could afford to do was sit a little aside for ourselves to sniff and try and sell the rest. He was under a lot of pressure, having to answer to somebody else. But he did what he had to do. Financial pressure started hitting us and we were losing money on the drug selling. We no longer had it like the big boys and it was due to our habits and freely treating others. We were using up so much of our drugs to get high twice a day and we had to stop.

I didn't want to hear that, so when he left to go to New York one day I told my friend to shoot me up like she was doing. My man did not allow people to shoot up in our house, but I needed to get high and I had only a little to sell, so my friend did it. She shot me up in the back of my arm, close to my elbow where you could not see it. Now I was on a roll. It felt good and it did not take much. I made her promise not to ever say anything and she told me not to worry. "You just don't say anything," she said, "and we will be cool or else they will be burying the both of us because that man is going to kill us both."

I kept this secret for a good six months when one day he sent me to New York for him because he had a real bad toothache. While I was there I shot up in front of some guys who went back and told him in front of everybody because they had had an argument. When he came home after everyone had left he asked about what had been said. I lied and he asked to see my arms. I showed him the front part and then he told me to raise up the back part of my arms. Man, my heart dropped. I was dead. He saw what he wanted and started beating on me with a roll of quarters and crying. I cannot repeat the names he called me and the things he said he was about to do. I ran out the house when I could get away but he followed me, hitting me the whole time. I saw a police car at the corner, watching our house, and I ran that way. He kept coming, saying he was from 'Nam and what are they going to do to him. He finally turned back and went to the house. I went to the house of a girl who lived on our street. She was a family friend but did not do drugs. She let me stay the night, and the next day I went to get my clothes. They were all over the yard. I went to my mother's house. She had our baby because he told her that he threw me out but needed her to watch our baby and he would pay her. She never knew why we fought but she told me to give it some time. "He needs to cool off," she said. "He loves you and this baby very much. "You had to do something really bad in order for him to go this far." At least he had not told her what happened.

The next weekend I was back at home with him but it was not the same. He was hurt and he could not trust me. We had been together since I was seventeen years old. Now I was twenty-one. I loved him but saw him in a different light, as well. He was crazy and he loved hard. He was an emotional, sick person when he was betrayed. One Sunday

I asked him if he would watch the baby while I went to the ice cream parlor to go with a neighbor who had asked me to accompany her. He liked her so he let me go but told me to hurry back before the baby woke up. We were about half the way back home when a car pulled up and someone called my name. I thought it was just one of our white drug customers. I kept walking. I knew not to go up to a car because you could get stuck-up that way. The car passed us and when we got to the corner of our house they were there waiting for me along with about nine other cars. They had arrested my baby's father and were about to take our baby when I told my neighbor to take my baby up the street to my niece's house and tell them I had gotten raided by the cops and was going to jail.

This was my first arrest and I was scared out of my mind. My baby's father kept yelling across the lock up, "Hang in there, baby. You'll be out in the morning." I could not sleep and my stomach kept turning. They brought my downstairs neighbor and friend to jail, as well, about an hour later. They said, "Look who else we have here to keep you company." I was not glad to see her locked up but I sure was glad for the company. I found out from her that they were doing a drug sweep and we were on their list to get raided. We went before the judge and I got the shock of my life. Everybody got out but me. They had a bench warrant out on me for selling drugs to an undercover agent. I did not know anything about going to the big house, but I was on my way. I had to have a lawyer, but we could not afford a big time lawyer. I told my mother where I had hidden a few bucks. She looked but said it wasn't there. The police had done a number on our apartment looking for more drugs and they may have found the money.

My oldest brother and my mother put money together to get me an attorney. They could not get me out on bond because it was too high. To be honest with you, I was caught red-handed because the pictures show it was me making a sell. I knew the agent as well. He went to school with my oldest brother, but went away to college and then started working his way through the police ranks. I had to go before the judge for a plea bargain. They wanted the guys that bring the drugs from New York into Connecticut, not me. I was a petty addict who they wanted as a snitch. I said, "Man, you must be out of your mind. Are you crazy? Not me." I spoke to my baby's father and I told him that I might have to go down for this. I can't give up anybody." That was the street code. I have seen snitches end up in the river with blocks on their feet. I never saw the big man but, believe me, there was one.

My lawyer said he was going to ask the judge to put me in a drug program, seeing that I had a habit and it was my first arrest. They really did not want me for two bags of drugs, but it was enough to make my life a living hell. I had women in jail with me who I used to baby sit for and they took me under their wings for my own protection. These were the gay women that I wrote about earlier. They were bad dope addicts. I was just a dope fiend. There was a difference. A dope addict did whatever they had to do to get high - sell their bodies, steal, rob, cashing someone else's check. It was not long before I learned all these new trades while waiting to go to trial. I read Psalm 91 every single day. My mother told me to read it out loud three times a day and I did. My mother was there to do her part as my mother, but she let me know I had a child that needed her mother. My baby's father was released from jail the next day. He brought my daughter to see me one time and, man, I could not handle it. I told him, my mother and brother not to ever bring her there again. They would search your kids, put their hands in the baby's pamper, talking about this is the process you have to go through in order to have a visit. My child had not done anything wrong so I refused to let them do that to her and allow her to be put to this type of shame on account of our wrongdoing.

I did not see my baby or him very much after that. He kept selling drugs, but I had my own issues to deal with. Nothing seemed to interest him or motivate him but me, so he just hung out and got more depressed and high. Finally, I had learn how to con people out of their money without them even knowing it until they were out of my sight. I learned how to boost clothes, very expensive clothes. These trades I learned only because I was bored. I really did not think I would ever use them but I did years later. Back at the court, the judge ruled in my favor that I be given a chance to change my life, especially when he learned that everybody around me was nine to twenty-six years older than me. He also took into account my schooling and my upbringing.

I went into a drug program. I could leave only if I was being discharged upon completing the program according to the directors there. I was sent to Fairfield Hills Hospital's drug unit. It was so pretty and green, way out from city living. I thought, man, maybe I could start over for my child's sake. At least I had to give it my best shot. With all the green grass and the lawns cut so nice, the air smelled so clean. I wanted to try to change and I put all my efforts into doing just that. I had a very hard time talking about myself and getting yelled at. Man, I would clean trash cans with my bare hands, but do not yell at me. I had such a violent temper and it kept me in trouble every single day. I was a set up for the other patients to get their privileges every weekend according to how many confrontation slips you dropped a week. It seemed like every week I had thirty or forty. I just could not handle being yelled at or told what to do. I could not trust anyone, especially those who said they cared a lot for me. Those liars I had to watch. How can you care about me when you don't even know me? "Stop lying" was always my response.

I was having so many temper problems that they threatened to send me back to jail if my behavior did not change. I wanted to change but I had become this out of control monster who could not stop herself from lashing out at people. I had this hidden fear of being hurt by them, and when they yelled I always went back to me being in the room with my mother and father yelling and her trying to cut him. One day I was asked if I wanted to meet with the unit psychiatrist. I said, "For what? I'm not crazy. You guys just need to realize that I'm not going to let you talk to me any way you want to." I was then told that the doctor wanted me as his client, so he would remain my one to one until further notice. He was very kind to me in every way. I took to him and he took to me. We used to go on long walks and just talk at first. Then he started family therapy stuff. I told him that my mother was not coming up there because she had a handicapped son at home. Besides that, she did not care about me being in there. She loved it because I was off the streets and out of her hair. She could sleep at night now. I told him she would not talk to him because she is going to feel like I'm telling our family business to white people. She would not see it as helping me iron out things in my head.

He asked a black counselor to sit in on the first session. To my surprise, my mother came and I let her talk first. She did just like I said she would. She blamed me, but that was ok. My turn came and I asked her why she never told me she loved me. She looked at me like I was crazy and said, "Is this what you brought me all the way up here for? I'm walking the floor every night with your child and you are going to ask me that?" Boy, I felt crushed. She thought taking care of my baby was showing me love, but I wanted her to say the words to me and she got angry and left, handing me a bag of shorts. I felt crushed, but at least I did it. Now they could move me up another level.

I was numb when it came to my personal feelings. This counselor asked me how I felt about what my mother had just done to me. I said, "It's cool, man. She has always treated me that way. The good part is that she is not hitting on me anymore. I can handle her running out like that." He asked me what did I think she heard me saying. I looked at him and I said, "Man, cut it. Don't even go there. How would I know what is going through her head?" I was glad I could move on in the program because some things you will never be able to fix, especially if the person does not believe anything is broken.

I gradually moved up into the phase of the program where I could go out on the grounds by myself. This helped my emotional state of mind because, as I shared earlier, I loved to be alone. It helped me to create a world of peace for myself, a world that I could control. I finally found myself because I had befriended this girl from Stamford who was in a relationship with my second shift staff member. I liked this staff member who told me to leave. We both had the same last name, so we would call each other "namesake". I left my baby's father alone because he helped to convince me that this was not a healthy relationship to go back to an active addict when coming out of a drug rehab center. I trusted him more than I did the other staff members, so I broke it off with my baby's daddy. It made sense. If I was going to change my life style then I needed to change the people I hang out with. Sadly, I later found out that he wanted me to himself for sexual purposes, nothing else. He fell in love with the wrong thing. I would sneak to his dorm at night on the weekend that he was scheduled to work. He would have me and my girl on the breakfast cart run. That meant that we both would have to be awakened by 5 am to shower, dress and get down in the tunnels by 5:30 am. The midnight shift staff would knock on our door to wake us up. He would not open the door but would call us by name. On the nights I stayed out, she would crack the door and say, "I'm up. I'll wake Carolyn up."

We had that thing down to a science. We never got caught, but his lies caught up with him. I did not tell on him. Rather, he told on himself. I found out that while he was out on his two-week vacation he was getting married. Boy, that hurt. But I was used to that sort of pain. I just thought that by now my life patterns were changing. But I was wrong. I was in the program and had gone to jail because I was trained by the street code that you never snitch on anyone. So, no, I did not tell on him.

My stomach would tie up in knots when he came on the unit after he got back. He said, "Carolyn, I missed you all the time I was gone. On my wedding night my mind was on you, girl. I'm really in love with you. I know I married the wrong woman, but I could not back out, I swear. I wanted to but there was nothing I could do. It was just too late." I looked at him and before I could open my mouth the voice from the madam that I used to go to the store for came to me along with these words: "it takes a poor 'ho' to lay on her back to make a dollar and if a man ever tells you he made a mistake when he married his wife, look that Negro straight in the eye and tell him 'No baby. She made a mistake when she swore her life to you." If a man does not know what he wants when he gets married, he will be forever looking for it or someone else to fulfill him. You will never have a good marriage. She said to let that liar go as soon as that lie comes out of his mouth, and that's just what I did. I asked him how he could be true to her if he didn't want her? I didn't want to know that for me. He needed to know that for himself.

Well, I walked off from the relationship, but he gave himself away by yelling at me on the floor. He kept getting on my case about everything, just like a child, and I finally told him that he needed to chill or he was going to be out of a job. Me, they would just send back to jail. He had a lot more to lose than I did. My one to one therapist asked me had my namesake shared any family problems with me. I knew staff were not to discuss personal issues with their clients, so I laughed and said, "Nothing other than being married. He's still is a little overwhelmed, I guess." "Well, what about the two of you?" he asked. "Your bonding with him seems to be going down hill and I thought everything was going great." Ok, this was a catch twenty two question. Do I play or stay? Finally, I responded, "Yeah, me too. But this guy is going off the hook every five minutes." He asked if this bothered me and I told him that it didn't and that maybe he felt he needed to get a little more tough with me to ensure that I didn't get too comfortable.

Later that week the staff had a long meeting. I could hear him yelling out but I couldn't tell what he was saying. After that meeting, the head administrator came out and called the house to attention. This is when all residents have to be present in the dining room area. When I arrived I heard him say that my namesake would be on to first shift effective immediately. I looked at him and I said to myself, "Yeah boy, they are going to be watching you now." I did not feel sorry for him because I knew he would have jammed me up sooner or later with this emotional fling thing going on in his head. How can you marry a person and think about some other women on your most important night? He was sick and, man, I needed to stay away from him, which I did, because two weeks after he came on first shift I was promoted to the last phase of the program. I could now seek a job. They even told me I could do full-time work. This had not been allowed before.

I got a full-time, second shift job at a factory, and I opened my own banking account. I got my driver's license and started to save money to buy a car. My life was truly on a positive note and was a great example to the program. However, things started to change. I had come up with a dirty urine test which I could not explain. Then, three weeks later, I had another dirty test. The staff called me in and told me I would have to give up my job and remain on the unit until they figured this thing out. I had more of the staff wondering how I could be so stupid to start using again, especially when I could be discharged in another four months. Then it occurred to two of the staff that I could only get the drugs when I was off campus. But my urine was dirty only on the weekend, and I did not take weekend passes. They then thought that someone might be switching bottle caps with me. I was the only patient there that would not go home, and I stayed to volunteer my time on the unit with the new girls.

So they watch the bottles and, sure enough, two male patients were changing my cap for their dirty urines. Thank God He cleared my name, or else I was headed for the jail cell. Those two guys didn't care about me going to jail. They just wanted to keep from getting kicked out. One guy they kicked out that same day. The other one shot himself in the foot the next weekend to cover up another drug high, but they asked for a drug test to be done on him and the hospital said he had tested positive for cocaine. So they both were out of the program in less than a week and a half. Before I left the program I wanted to have a car. I had enough money saved up but I still needed a co-signer. Can you believe my therapist signed for me to get my first car? Man, I was so glad I had to make payments to the bank. My therapist said to keep it to myself because he could not go around doing that sort of thing all the time, but he felt good about trusting me to be responsible.

After I got out, I stayed in the Newtown and Danbury area, working and saving up my money. My baby's father supported her along with his other daughter, so I was told. I only know for sure that he gave my mother twenty five dollars at the end of every week until I started to get more letters from home saying, "Hi. How are you? Mama told me to write you and to let you know that she has not heard from nor seen the baby's father in two weeks and he owes her fifty dollars. She wants her money or else one of you have to come and get her or she is going to call the state people on both of you." Now, my mother knew there was no need to write me at a program that she knew I could not leave until the weekend, so I would call and tell her that I would be home on the weekend. I told her that because I had to work on Saturday mornings, I could meet her at about 2:00 p.m. I went to my therapist to tell him what I had going on in Bridgeport and he said, "Fine, Carolyn. I believe this is a great move for you. It's great we can work on your family issues from this stand point. How did your visits go with your daughter? How does your mom see the change in you? Hopefully, this will get her support." I looked at this very nice, caring, but naïve, Indian man and said to myself, "All this knowledge you have and not a bit of common knowledge to help you along." He got up, hugged me and said, "Cheer up, Carolyn. There are only good things for you now. You are doing a wonderful job here. We all love you."

I agreed to go home that weekend. My first pass and, man, was I nervous. After leaving work I drove straight home to Bridgeport, stopping first at my mom's house. Only two of my sisters and my baby brother in the wheelchair were there. They were a little shy of me and standoffish, but I understood. I had been gone for about seventeen months, but I had spoken to them on the phone during that time. I could sense their uneasiness so I asked for my baby. They said that my mother took her with her downtown that morning and she should be back in a hour or so. I then decided to go up the block to see if I could locate the baby's father, and I told them to tell my mother where I had gone. As I was walking up the street I started to get nervous, so I began to talk to myself: "Its been a while. Black folks are still standing in the same spot you left them in. Oh, well. You are different now. Keep walking." So I did.

Two blocks up the street I ran into just who I needed to see to get to where my baby's father was now living - his best friend. I was glad to see him and he was glad to see me as well. I asked him for my baby's father and he had a stupid look on his face. He started to tell me that he was glad to see me and he knows my baby's dad will be as well, but he wanted me to wait so he could go get him for me. Then he told me not to be surprised by what he looks like. After waiting about twenty minutes neither one showed up so I left to go back to my mother's house. On the way I ran into one of my running partners. She was glad I was out and wanted to hookup and party that night, but I thanked her and said, "No, thank you. I'm only home to check in on my baby and find out what's the deal with her daddy. Let my mother tell it, he has not been around to see her or sent any money in three weeks now." She said, "Girl, listen to me. I would not tell anybody else this but you." (She was lying. This girl told everybody's business. She couldn't hold ice if she was a refrigerator.) She went on to tell me that my baby's father was a strung-out junkie selling blow whenever he could spare it. She said that you could put your arm around his whole body, that's how bad he looked from shooting drugs. Also, the word was that he was sleeping around with our best girlfriend. That one was hard to believe, but a couple of nights I did see them arguing about money on the corner where he lives.

I asked her where he lived and she said, "Girl, the house you just walked past is your daughter's father's house, where every junkie on this side of town runs in and out." The she said, "Girl, he done went down to nothing. Everybody said when you get back that man is going to spring back up because you was always about making that money. You kept him on his feet. Now she is taking him to the cleaners. What little he gets, she gets it first." I felt so sick to my stomach. I asked what in the world happened, and she told me that he couldn't make it on his own and needed a strong woman like me to keep her foot on things and set the pace for him.

I felt bad, knowing that quitting him over the phone was not a good thing for me to have done. He never really had anyone to care for him but me. It was always the two of us, no matter what. I told her that we had not been together for about nine months and that I had even messed around on him in the program. But I loved my baby's father, and if I could help him get into a program I would. She laugh at me and said, "You and I both ended up with two nuts that have never been deprogrammed from the war and you want him to go to a program. Girl, you need some get high yourself talking like that. He isn't doing no program. The army killed any change that could have ever been done for any of those Vietnam vets. They are all strung out on something or locked up. They can go for free and not one of them will even talk about it. No, you need to march your behind up there and get your man and help him before someone kills him up there. He got jumped the other night and nobody would help him. I felt sorry for him. You should see his face."

I told her that I had sent his boy to get him for me but he never came back to say anything. She told me he lived on the second floor of the building I had just passed and had the whole side for himself. I found out they were trying to evict him, but he wouldn't leave. How did he get an apartment and not pay rent? She told me that the landlord had used him to do a job but, because he was a junkie, would not pay him as much as he would have paid someone for the same job. My baby's father was not going for it and told the landlord he would burn the building down if he tried to mess with him. So, the landlord left him alone.

I thanked her for the information and I started to walk off. I needed to see my baby first. Besides, I didn't want to hear my mother's mouth. I had changed but she hadn't. Upon arriving at the house I heard my baby. I ran upstairs but my mother grabbed her, put her in the house and shut the door. I said, "What are you doing? Open the door." Then my mother said, "No. You are not coming in here with your drunk self." I told her that I wasn't drunk and that I had gone up the street only to find the baby's father and ended up talking to an old friend and coming straight back to her house. Then she told me she had heard I was working and wanted to know why I hadn't sent some money home for the baby. "That little bit of scratch he gives me don't feed no baby," she said. I told her that twenty-five dollars a week for a two and a half year-old was enough, especially since he also bought her diapers and food. "What more do you want from him," I asked. She thought he could be doing more for this kid if he was not out there shooting dope. I said, "Well, that's not your problem to worry about. As long as he is doing her don't you be concerned about what he shoots."

I felt the web being woven around my heart and it was beginning to hurt. So I said, "Look, Mama. I did not come down here to argue with you. Let me please see my baby so I can get back to the program." She asked if I was planning on leaving some money her for the baby and I told her I could write a check because we were not allowed to carry cash in the program. Well, she didn't like that. "If you knew that then why didn't you bring some money with you. I got to pay my tithes in church tomorrow." I said, "Here, I'll make it out to my oldest brother, Mama. He can get it cashed. Trust me. And give the girls ten dollars as well." I told them that mama had ten dollars for them both for school snacks. They said "thank you" and ran back in the room.

I wrote a check for eighty dollars and handed it to my mother. She told me to put it on the table, as if I had roots on me. I said, "Mom, you know sometimes I just don't understand you. I'm sorry. I try but I just don't. "She said, "You are not supposed to understand me. If you had listened to me and kept you're a___ at college you wouldn't be in the mess you're in now. A jail bird. All that knowledge you have. You're just stupid. Your daddy wasn't nothing and you never will be. Just go. She's your child. Get back to where you need to be. If them white folks up there knew like I know they would have been threw you out."

I hardly had any time to visit with my baby. She was so pretty, growing tall and thin, just like her daddy. She favored his side of the family, but she had my eyes, my smile and a head full of thick hair. Boy, she was beautiful. It was time for her to take a nap. She started to cry and I gave her to my sister to put down for a nap. I said "goodbye" to everyone and I left. I didn't know which way to go. My first pass home in eighteen months and all I got was a kick in the heart. I hurt so bad on the inside I just could not think. I remember them telling us to look at the positive things that happened in your day and how you handled everything that was negative or hurtful. I did all that. I could do those things, but old pain kept coming up. I wanted to go back to the program and say, "Please don't make me go back." But I felt ashamed of how that would be seen. Everyone there was so glad I was going out, especially the staff. They had helped so much and I could tell that they were proud of me. So I stayed in that mindset for a few moments and I calmed down enough to think clearer for the moment. Stay in the moment. Sometimes all you have is that moment to hang on to.

I rode around the city. I picked up a grinder, ate it in my car and tried real hard not to think about anything that had happened at my mother's house. I just tried to eat and waste some time. I wanted to see my daughter's father before I left. I rode by there that night around 7:00. I saw him going into that building, but I only saw him from the side. I went around the block to park and took the back stairs. I wanted to surprise him. I needed to take a shower, as well. I had been in the same clothes all day and this just was not my style. I knocked on the door and some dude who did not know me from Adam's housecat opened the door. He was high and thought I sounded like some chick that had just left there. I asked for my baby's father by name and he said, "Oh, you must be his woman from out of town. Mama, I don't think you want to see him right now. He is all busted up. He got jumped last night or the night before, so let me just give you a heads up, ok? I thanked him but told him I could handle things from there, and then he told me where his room was.

I started to walk. The place gave me the chills, but I had been in worse places in New York city. So I knocked on the bedroom door. He said, "Everything you need is in the back so you better need change to pay my man if you made your way back here," and he pulled back the sliding doors. I just stood there. When he looked up and saw me he asked, "Why did you come up here? I know I owe your mom and I'm working on it right now. If I wanted you to see me looking like this I would have come downstairs this morning, Carolyn. My boy told me you were downstairs. Now go. I don't want to see you here ever again. There is no need in you coming back here. There is nothing here for you. Go on with your life and keep your head like always. Smell life for yourself. Leave this building. Go, girl, while you can." I said, "No, I'm not leaving you because you would never leave me like this. There is no way we could spend as many years as we have together and I leave you. Look at your face all busted up, your eye closed on one side. Baby, how can you say you can make it. You can't even see. No, you don't need me, but I need to help you." He cried and said he was tired but this is where drugs had brought him to.

He never mentioned to me about my best friend sleeping there with him in the same bed, so when she came in about an hour later he looked at me and said, "You need to go now because she has to get some rest." "What did you just say to me," I asked. He said, "I told you earlier to move on with your life. This is no life for you." My best friend smiled and he said to her, "Don't play games with her; this is my baby's mother. No one comes before her and there will never be one for me after her." He then told me that my best friend hustled and sometimes dropped by to crash at his place when she couldn't make it home. He would let her use his bed to crash in until daylight. I told him I still needed to talk to him and he said to come back the next day. So, I left.

I felt hurt but it was a cold hurt inside. Most people would think it would make some women happy to hear a man say that she is the only person he will ever love, but it saddened me. Something was ending, but what I didn't know. I smelled death in that room that day, like a dark, cold-blooded odor. I came back the morning after I slept in my car. I parked up the street from his house where a lot of cops kept driving by. I got a few winks here and there, but I was ok. When I went back that next morning he would not open the door. I kept being told that he was sleeping and to come back at five o'clock. I said, "Tell him it's his baby's mother." The guy said, "He knows it's you, but he is taking care of some important business right now."

I felt bad, so I called his mother. I told her everything. She asked me to wait and show her the house so that she and her husband could come back later and get him and at least move him to the old family house where we lived after I had the baby. So I agreed to wait. This was the least I could do. You see, my baby's father was so much older than me. They never really blamed me for what he did. They just said they were sorry I had to go through this because of their son. This came from his mother. His father never said more than two words year after year - hi and bye. He was weird, always saying nothing and just very quiet. I met her and showed her the building where he live and what floor he lived on. She told me I looked good, to take care of myself, and not to be a stranger. Then I pulled off. This was my first visit to Bridgeport, my home, in eighteen months.

I wished many a day they had kept me locked up in that program after what I experienced next. One weekend I went home after getting off of my in-house restrictions and my mother started in on me about my baby. I could tell that getting back my daughter from her was going to be like a nightmare from hell. I asked if I could take her out to the store and bring her back right before she takes her nap. Her response was, "How would you know when she gets put down for her nap? While you up there, laying around in that program I have been here walking the floor every night with your crying baby." I said, "Mom, I'm not going down this road with you every time I come home. I just asked you a simple question and the answer is yes or no." "You have not brought a dime home," she argued, "and that addict father of hers has not been here to see her but just sends the money and a note to tell my baby daddy loves her. I told my mom that she was getting her money on time and I wasn't going to keep giving her money every time I come home just to be able to see my baby. She was only going to get what was agreed upon between her and him. I wanted to be left out of it. Then I told her, "Besides, as many of your babies and the neighbor's kids as I have kept, I can basically tell when a child needs a nap. Mama, come on now. You just want to fuss and I'm not going there with you."

I turned to walk off and she started hitting me with the handle of a broom like a mad woman. The kids were yelling at her to stop and not to hurt me. I could hear them just before I mentally caved in. I had to get out of the back door. She was hitting me in my back and upside my head really hard. When I left home I said nobody was going to beat on me again, so I felt a rage coming. I saw red and it became dark. I knew I was ok because I did not hear her any more. Was I really ok? No, emotionally my life and all the changes I had made went to hell. I did not care because no one else cared. It seemed like a game was being played with my life. It seemed like this was how my life was supposed to be, so why change and for whom? The judge did not know me or what I had been through my whole life thus far.

My body and my head ached with pain. Man, I tried to talk to my baby's daddy, but he told me to go on where I came from. I looked good, but he had what he wanted and it sure was not tearing down my life along with his. We talked for a long time and I could not see past that moment with him. I told him to go to a detox program but he told me to worry about myself. He was just fine and he would be like this always, he told me. He gave me a hug and said, "Girl, if you stay away from that crazy mother of yours you'll do just fine. You two are too much alike." I asked him what he was going to do about himself. He needed to be in a program. He again told me not to worry about him. He could handle it. He always loved me, but drugs can tear down the strongest bond.

I left him standing outside the gate of the old family house of theirs and I walked around the neighborhood. Everyone wanted to know if I was out or just visiting. I replied each time that I wasn't coming back there to stay and that I was just visiting my family. Boy, that word hurt, but not as much as when some of the older neighbors would say, "I know your mama is really proud of you. You have left that mess alone and gone on to change your life." Now that hurt because she had just beat me to a pulp. I smiled and kept walking, not realizing that I had nowhere to go and that I did not belong anywhere. I wanted to cry, but tears just weren't there. I thought about my father but he just wasn't there. I just walked and hurt. Then I decided to return back to my car. It was dark. Now, I could move it from in front of my mother's house. I drove back to the program in silence, asking God when this life would be over and will life always have to be so full of pain.

I arrived back two hours early, checked in, gave up a urine sample and went to bed, only to toss all night long. However, it was over by morning. I shared with my one to one what had happened but only on a surface level. He told me he could have the matter in court before five that afternoon, but I wasn't going to take my mother to court. He asked me what I wanted him to do and I told him that he had done all he could do. I had done what they asked me to do and I now knew about making good choices and bad choices. I knew that if i ever stuck a needle in my arm again that I was the one that made that choice, nobody else. So what more was there for them to do? He looked very disappointed but what I told him was the truth. At the same time, I was pushing him away in order to take my next step into the drug world.

I experienced an emotional break down a week later and walked off the premises of the program without permission. I even got a ride with a staff member, which put his job in danger. But I had lost it, and neither he nor I realized it. What happened was I was no longer on his level of the program and they sent me out to get the mail. I had not returned, but they trusted me. It never crossed their minds that I would try to escape. Well, I did escape, but I had missed the bus and was walking. I never told the staff any better. My mother was notified and she would not let me in, of course. I had shamed the family. I just wanted my world to stop hurting, but it kept on moving, spinning me like a web I could not get out of.

I spent the night with my baby's father and saw the horrible things he was doing to himself. Now he was shooting drugs in his groin. That wasn't going to be me, baby. When veins die they are dead. I asked him what in the world he was thinking. He got angry and cursed me. I left because if the drugs make you do that to yourself, what would they make you do to me? I started hanging out in the after hour clubs when the bars closed. I stood in hallways or lived in them until I found out there was a warrant out for me and I turned myself in. You see, after I went on the run in 1975 I ran to Columbia, South Carolina. I thought every cop car was looking for me. At that time I had never been to jail and I sure did not want my first time going to jail to be in the south. So I returned and turned myself in. Here I go again, I thought. But they were cool. They let me be a drug counselor/aide at a program in Waterbury. I would get the girls up for school and take them to their evening appointment. It was nice. I was supposed to be there for one year, but the director and his crew got busted for having sex with the young girls in his house. One girl even took the police to his house and told the cops where he had hidden a pair of her panties and some pictures he had taken of her. Well, it had all come out, and seeing that they were going to close down the program, I was free to go home.

I had no where to go once I got there because I wasn't doing drugs at that time, but that did not last after I got back to Bridgeport. I went home, hoping to be able to stay there until I could find somewhere to live, but that did not work out at all. I couldn't ever say anything about how to raise my own child. It was like I wasn't even there. I could not take her anywhere. So the fussing and noise in my head started again, and off to the street I went. I went back to getting high, but I promised myself I would never move back home to stay. I could not live by my mother's rules so I had to, once again, find my own way. Again, I slept in hallways and stayed on the streets in the winter as well as the summer. I tried to sell drugs again, but it was not the way it used to be. So I became my own customer. That lasted about four months and I was off and running again, trying to stay ahead of the street life.

I did not want people to talk about me like they were about other girls on the street, so I used my head and I learned how to become a street doctor. That is a person who shoots drugs into someone who can't find a vein or was too sick to do it themselves. How did I learn this? Well, while I was in New York there was a guy that used to come up to the shooting gallery and he would have a book with him that had a map of the human body. He was well-dressed, so I knew he had to work out of a hospital or lab. I watched him as he would lay out that book and look at the veins. He followed it until he located the place on his body where you could not see the tracks. Then he would get high, close his book, and leave. I thought to myself, "I can do that," so I learned and got paid to get people "off" or high. They would pay me or give me drugs in return. It did not matter to me.

I spent a lot of time on the stroll at night, working with the street girls to keep them high so they could make their money. But that got to be a hassle waiting around in the cold then sometime they went with other people so I had to be sick and make money other ways. I used to pretend to want to sleep with a guy and then tell him I was sick. He would buy me drugs and then I would run off. Boy, I played that one for a long time. I even shot drugs in front of them just to scared the heck out of them. They would say, "Never mind, baby. I've got to go meet up with some friends. I'll catch up with you later." That one worked a lot.

I used to go over to the projects and work out of one of the shooting galleries for the night. I would get high, have a place to crash and would have money to get high for the next day. But that only worked on the first of the month when state checks came out. Now listen. I am only telling my story, not someone else's. I did enough of my own mess. I do not need to tell someone else's story. I say this to say that I did not believe in taking food out of people's children's mouths, but sometimes when you are sick you do what you have to do. I did not shoot drugs in new addicts. I just did not want to start someone new on that rode to hell. I would not get pregnant women high. That was a rule of the streets. Some people would do it, but I did not go there.

I was on the food stamp program and I sold my stamps to buy drugs. I slept in abandoned buildings and after hours clubs only because I did not want to go back home. I would hear that my brothers were looking for me, but I would hide in another part of town. Sometimes they would find me and talk to me or curse me out. They were ashamed of me and I could not blame them, but I told them that this was my life. Nobody tried to help me when I was at home, so I didn't need their help now. I knew I could not stop myself. I was too far gone, so there was no need to hide from them or anyone else that once knew me. Church people, especially those from my mother's church, would ride by and shake their heads or just turn their heads as they rode past. Everybody judged you and nobody wanted to talk to you.

I remember once calling the pastor of our church because he said he was there for us young folks. And he was there for you if you were willing to be with him. I'm not saying that he tried to sleep with me, but I knew him and we were not on the same page when I met him that night. I was not feeling what he was feeling. Or should I say his "vibe" was not to help me but himself. He never approached me directly, but I knew and he knew we were not on the same page. I would never say a man of God put himself out on me, especially if he was not direct about it, but a few months later he was asked to step down for so many reasons. I believe his looks and his flesh got the best of him. The last I heard he had a church in Atlanta.

I could not trust the church to help me. I just did not like the way they treated me, but I still prayed every day. I started to drink more and more and shoot drugs less because my veins were wearing out. It was hard to get a hit and I was tired of having to stand out on the streets in the cold every night for hours. Once in a while, I could feel my feet going from wet to frozen. I would go to my niece's mother's house and she would feed me, let me take a hot shower or bath, and let me sleep until I was ready to get up, eat and leave. She loved me very much. That much I know. She and her sisters saw past my faults and met my needs. They knew how my mother treated me. They always tried to stop my pain, but they couldn't. I was too afraid to let anyone into my heart. I did whatever they told me to do when I was with them, but once I was out of their sight I had to hold it down for myself.

That same year, upon my return from Waterbury, my daughter's father died. Man, nobody ever told me about that kind of pain. My best friend had just died. My protector had just died. My first lover had just died, and my cold world became colder. I went to the funeral and my baby was there. She kept coming over to me and climbing in my lap. They kept taking her away like I had some type of germ. I knew my family did not know anything about the drug world other than what they had read in the papers and saw on the news, so I allowed for some of their stupidity. But this took the cake. I asked my sister why she kept running over and taking the baby down from my lap. She said, "Do you think that I like what has happened to you? Look at you, girl. You were so pretty. Everybody used to talk about how fine you were. Now look at you. I feel sorry for you so I brought your baby hoping that, at least, you could see her. But mama told me I better not let you touch her or take her anywhere, so I've got to do what I'm told. You know how mama can get. Look at how many beatings you took for me. I'm scared of mama. You don't have to live there anymore, but I do. So be grateful for what I was able to get done and please don't take this child from here."

I could feel the fear and the love for me all at once. I assured her I would never ever put her life in harm's way and told her I loved her and our sisters very much and to please finish high school at least. I asked her to please take care of my baby for me and that I would not come and get her. I was too sick with the drugs anyway. A tear fell from her charcoal eyes. She was very dark-skinned compared to me, but oh so beautiful. "You're a pretty black girl," I would always tell her. She had developed a nervous condition as a result of living at home and seeing all the violence that took place. I took her under my wing and promised her long ago that nobody would ever hurt her, and I lived up to my word to the point of almost killing a man with a bat because he hit her. I was a fighter. It did not matter if you beat me up. I was coming back until I won.

I left my baby's father's mother's house that night and I don't remember too much after that. For quite some time, I lost track of life. Well, the living and breathing part of it anyway. I just roamed from one day to the next. When I woke up it was spring time. I had a drinking problem along with the drugs and I was now twenty-six years old. I lived with a man who I could not stand. We used to party every weekend, drinking non-stop. I asked him one day how in the world did I end up with you. He laughed and I said, "No, really. What in the world do you want with me?" I knew it was the sex, but I wanted the truth. He was not man enough to tell me and it was cool.

I finally got myself together and got a job. I had a paycheck coming in every week and, bam, I found out I was pregnant. I told him and he said he didn't want any children. I didn't want any either, so I had an abortion. After I got back from the clinic I found out that he had told everybody in the bar where we hung out. When I walked in they were looking at me like I shot their mother or something. Then my girl, who was the barmaid, called me in the bathroom and told me what he had done. To them, he had acted as if he really wanted the baby. This man was a punk, and still is in every aspect of the word. I got drunk that night and I stayed out all weekend for the first time in a long time. This man wanted to make me look like a monster so he could feel like a man. Boy, I wanted to kick his behind, but I needed a place to stay. I went to my niece's mother's house and I told her what had happened. Again, she made me feel alive. She told me that God would forgive me and to never, ever, do that again.

A month later I was six-weeks pregnant, and I had to keep this man's baby. My mother found out and asked me why would I want to bring a baby into this world being born an addict. I looked at her and remembered that thing she did to me when I was fifteen years old came rushing back. Boy, I took off. I did not know what to do, but I knew what not to do. One day I was sitting in the bar and this tall man I used to see in the bar was in there alone with the barmaid. He looked at me as I walked in and he said to the barmaid, "Put your hands over your ears for a moment. I need to say something to this woman right here and I do not want you to hear me." We laughed and he said, "No, I'm serious about this. Please." So she covered her ears and he called me a "dumb, stupid b_____." I looked at him and he said, "Look at you. I never would have believed you would let life throw you a wrench of any kind and you not fight like hell to get out of it. What went wrong? I watched you as a child growing up through struggle after struggle just to finish high school, and you rose above every obstacle just to get to here an die? You make me sick." I was numb to his words, but I still asked, "What brought this about?" He said, "You, throwing your life away like this." I asked what my life had to do with him and he grabbed me by my arm and said, "I'm going to show you."

He pushed me out of the bar and into his car. He then drove me down the street to a rooming house. I asked him what he was doing and who lived at the house. He rang the doorbell and a short man came to the door. He said to the short man, "Give her the key and nobody besides her is allowed to stay here." I asked him what he was talking about and he said, "This is a place for you to stay until you have that baby. If you want that child to grow up being addicted then you continue to use those drugs. If not, I will take you to the clinic in the morning to sign up for methadone." I didn't know why he was doing this. I only knew him from going to school and seeing him pass us on the street. So I asked, "What is in this for you?" He said, "There are people who care about you, believe it or not." Right. Someone was just going to rent a room for me, pay my medical expenses for detox and then want nothing in return? That was kind of hard to believe. He then began to tell me about how the guy I was with had been talking about me like I needed him and like he was doing me a favor. This man said, "You tell him to kiss you where the sun don't shine. You don't have to live like that. Besides, he's going to get married in June." I said, "June? That's when my baby is due." He said, "Buttercup, he is not marrying you; that man is engage to another woman. So you are going to need this place real soon. I know you don't have any money, so I'm offering to help you get on your feet." I was in shock. It wasn't that I loved this baby's father, but why would he want to make my life any worse off than it was? I approached him with all this information, but he lied.

I took off to live by myself in that room. At least I was not on the streets. My new friend brought me money for food and took me to the clinic every morning before going home to his wife. Man, these guys' lives were more messed up than mind. But there was one guy there who only wanted someone to talk. He needed a person to listen and he would talk for hours. After we talked he would get up and leave. He never touched me or even tried. I thought that if I wasn't carrying that idiot's baby this guy would be a nice catch. He was about thirteen years older than me, but I have never had a boyfriend my age. This man cared so much for me. It seem like he did everything for me and I knew it wasn't going to last. Nothing good ever did.

I was shooting a lot of cocaine by now due to the fact that methadone will not allow you to feel heroin. Coke is what works good with methadone. My baby was born on June 7, 1980. Her father got married that same day. He came to the hospital all dressed in a blue tux and looked to make sure this baby was his. I was dealing with being depressed and going through withdrawal at the same time. I could not handle the drugs they were giving me and now this nut comes to the hospital parading in his tux. I just lost it, man. I waited until visiting hours were over that night and the nurses were returning the babies to the nursery before I walked out of the hospital, leaving my baby girl there.

I walked to the shooting gallery and had as much coke as I could get for free. I went back to the avenue where I hung out. The streets were on fire. Everybody was looking for me because I had walked out of the hospital. I called my friend. He was the only person left that I could trust. He said he would be right there and told me not to let anyone see me and not to go to the room. He was going to pick me up at my niece's mother's house or somewhere in that area. I did as he told me and he came and got me. I told him I didn't know what happened. They gave me all those drugs at the hospital and then they let that jerk up there in his wedding clothes. I was all mixed up. I didn't mean to leave the hospital but I couldn't think. He held me in his arms for the first time and I fell asleep in his car. When I woke up it was daybreak. He had sat up all night while I slept and he told me that everything was going to be alright.

We went to my mother's house and he went in to talk to her. When he came out he was upset. He said, "Man, I cannot believe that mother of yours. But at least she will let you stay here with the baby until I find you apartment." I did not want that but, hey, I wanted my baby. The only way to get her back was if I agreed to stay with my mother until I got a place of my own and if DCF felt I was doing well in the outpatient care drug program. I went with my mother to bring my daughter home. Everybody fell in love with her. She had fair skin and very pretty. God had truly had blessed me with healthy children considering all the drugs I was doing. They were not drug positive and I thank God for this miracle in my children's lives.

My mother did not waste any time throwing in my face the fact that I had walked out of the hospital and left my child behind. Every day I heard this and every day for four months she told me when to go, where to be, and when to wake up and feed my baby. She called me name after name after name. Then one day I just took off, not planning to ever return. I gave my daughter a bath and laid her in the middle of my mother's bed so she wouldn't fall off. I took a long shower, trying to wash her voice out of my skin and cleaned myself of all the name calling over the years, but it did not work. I got out of the shower, put on my clothes, climbed out the bathroom window and took off down the hill. I called my friend who told me he had to work later but to go to the bar and tell our friend to give me money until that night, which I did. I bought liquor and cocaine. I had taken my methadone that morning, and that combinations caused me to pass out from an overdose. Some friends from the streets helped bring me around. I did not remember anything until they told me. After I had that overdose you would think I would give up, but no. Two months later I overdosed in the bar. They asked me not to come back because it was bad for their business. They hated to do me that way, but I understood. I was on death row and I did not need any company.

I finally ended up sleeping with my friend who had been taking care of me through my pregnancy. He did not push himself on me. It was what I wanted and he did not turn me down. He loved me. This I knew more than I can express but he had a family. He did not want his wife, just his kids. I thought they were through because he told me she had filed papers, which I saw. But after we moved in together, she dropped it and wanted to try to work things out. He loved me, but I was unstable and so was he. I asked why he would want a life with someone like me. He had a good job and a family already, but he looked at where it was all going and said he was not in the picture for his family. His wife was more focused on the kids and there was no real love and caring between him and his wife. My friend and I stayed together for over ten years, but I put that man through hell. He continued to take care of me and we had a daughter together, as well. Now I had three girls. With my drug habit I was unable to keep any of them on my own.

Let me back up for a moment. Before I had my third daughter I was living in the streets again. After I left my mother's house, leaving my two daughters there with her, I started drinking heavily again and getting back into the club scene. I would get drunk and call the cops on myself just to get a ride home to the projects down the street from where my mother lived. We could do this back in the eighties because of all the prostitutes being killed. See, around this time they were finding girls strangled in the parks, so we had a city alert for women in the city to get a ride home late at night on the weekends instead of hitchhiking. So I used this for my benefit to get from one side of town to the other on the weekends. I would just say where I lived and that I could not locate my ride and I could take a cab or if a cop car was in that area they would take you. People said I was crazy but it got me where I needed to be. I stopped that game after getting beat up by two white cops one night. I was drunk and I only remembered half of both their badge numbers, but the police in the area knew me well and they knew I was not lying. Still, they swept it under the rug.

I used to sleep in abandoned buildings along with the wine heads. They all lived in the basement of this bootleg preacher's old building. He kept it clean down there and every wine head in the neighborhood had a little cubical in the basement to sleep in. They each had a little cot and there was a stove and two bathrooms down there, like they were really going to take a shower in that cold water. Unfortunately, he used these people. He got their city checks every Saturday and took out his portion of money. He gave them enough money to buy wine, but that was it until the next weekend. He took a portion of their food stamps and said he was making sure the dope heads were not going to come and rob them. Sure, we would take a few stamps, but we looked out for them and they looked out for us. But this preacher? He was just down right dirty. I would go down there some nights when I was really tired. I would get high and just sit in front of the stove or just wrap up in my coat and lay across one of their beds. Don't get me wrong. I had morals. My mother taught me how to take care of myself. I had good hygiene and I stayed clean. I would go to the bar and take a bath early in the morning when my friend came to clean the bar for the owner. I would wash myself up really good and then go to the church clothing bank to get some clean clothes for that day. They knew me and gave me whatever

I needed. I ate lunch at the soup kitchen. Sometimes I would be drunk before 10:00 in the morning and have to sleep it off and I would miss the soup kitchen. So I drank my dinner, as well.

My friend who I had stopped seeing came back around after he had gotten over me leaving the place where he had arranged for me to stay in order to get me off the streets. I just did not want anybody doing anything for me anymore and I have to pay it back in trade. He did not set things up to look like that, but it was the same with him. He just had a slicker way of getting what he wanted than the other lowlife. I was just tired of people seeing my body before they saw me as a person, but nobody understood that or wanted to hear it. Sex was all they thought about, and I was not going down like that. Sorry, but I did have a little pride left.

I had my way with men. I had a mailman friend that I hooked up with who gave me people's income tax checks. I would cash them and we would split the money. I stole clothes and food. Whatever your order was, if I could steal it for you, then I did. I had a group of friends that I ran with only for that purpose. An old lady out of New York who called herself "Mama" taught me how to boost with a long line girdle, the kind that went down your leg. She would take me in to large liquor stores, the ones where you would call and order champagne for the evening. She would order these wines and champagne that her boss wanted ready for pickup. The man would run in the back to get these because they were expensive drinks and he could tell someone rich had sent us. I'm sure he thought we must work for the rich white people in Westport or Greenwich, Connecticut. It was funny to see how these people would run to get these orders when they heard the names she was rattling off. While they were in the back she would grab two gallons of the alcohol on our list. She would give some to me and we would shove the alcohol in our girdles and walk like two ducks right out the store. If the store buzzer went off she would say, "I've got to get the check out of the car. I'll be right back," and we would take off. I did not like this kind of boosting, but it made good money. It's just that it was an all day job. Plus, this old lady had a lot of game with her. You would help her steal, but she wanted most of the money. So, I had to cut her loose. That old lady would have made me hurt her for sure.

I started stealing and cashing food stamps and selling them to side stores that were in the buying business. However, I stopped that because the feds were on it and I had a chance to walk away with out any problem, so I let that go. I then started to do "snatch and grab" robberies with some other girls, but they were low down, as well, and I let them go. Then one day I looked around and I saw that I needed to leave all this mess alone. I had no veins and I was shooting cocaine in my neck at this time. I was on death row. I got locked up for stealing and then got out on probation. I went to detox and met some really nice nurses there. I stayed there twenty-eight days and when I got out I was drunk the same night. I decided to go to my family doctor to ask him for some help. My arms were swollen from constantly missing the veins while shooting up, and I needed some antibiotics for the swelling. I got an appointment for a Saturday morning but I did not see him until about noon. I was feeling bad, but I did not know at the time that he had patients ahead of me. So, I kept going to the desk. The receptionist told me that he was behind but he knew I was there and asked that I please wait. I waited and finally got to see my family doctor, the man I had been crying to and treated by since I was eleven years old. I told him what had been going on and he listened for a few minutes. Then he got up and told me to lift up my blouse. He supposedly listened to my lungs and then all of a sudden he sucked my breast. I froze and then said, "What in the world is wrong with you? Who in the hell do you take me for?" He said he was sorry but that he had heard so much about me and my street life and thought we could help each other out. I said, "Help each other out?" I cannot write what I said after that but, baby, he was too through with me and I was done with him. Still, I did not let his office or anyone else know what he had done.

I called my friend and he came to pick me up from the diner down the street from the doctor's office. My friend was mad but I told him to let it go. That was just how things had been for me so far. Everybody saw my body but not me. My friend claimed he did not look at me that way, but as soon as I moved in with him he wanted to keep me as a prisoner. I had plenty to eat and all that and we went to the movies and to the club together, but I stayed home while he worked. Or so he thought. I started sneaking out on him while he worked. I would get high and by the time he made it home I was showered and fixing his dinner or little snack. One night, I snuck out while he was asleep. It was raining. I only wanted to go cop some coke, but this white dude offered me a ride to the 'hood to get better coke, so I took the ride. After getting into the car he pulled a knife on me and put it to my throat. I could not see it at first, but I could feel it. Man, I was scared. I started to pray and then I asked him if he wanted the money. He said, "No, I'm going to rape you, b_____ then kill you." I said to myself, "Oh my God. This is the guy they are looking for who's been killing the street girls. Oh Jesus. Oh my God. I'm going to die for sure now." That's all I can remember saying. Then I saw that knife. I had never seen one that big. I said to myself, "Well, if I'm going to die it won't be without a fight." I grabbed the door and tried to open it, but no luck. I kept trying and he kept locking it. Then I got mad (or so scared) that I grabbed the knife and he pulled it as he was struggling to control the car. He was taking me to this beach area, but I was not going down without a fight.

I was bleeding but could not feel my hand because, I later learned, he had cut the nerves. We kept struggling in that car, but a few minutes later a car came toward us and he panicked. It looked like a cop car checking the area, but it was actually a security guard. I didn't matter to me, because this nut tried to ram the car into the security car and this was when I jumped out of the car. I got the license plate number before busting my head against the high curb. I ran to the security guard who did not want to give me a ride. I said, "Man, that guy tried to kill me." I told him to take me to a certain hospital, but he ended up taking me all the way across town to another one. However, that was ok because God had worked it out so that a doctor was there operating on a state trooper. If he would be willing to treat my hand I would not lose my left thumb. God gave me favor with this doctor and he stitched my thumb back on using only local anesthesia. He could not put me to sleep because of that stupid methadone program. It hurt so bad, but a nurse held my hand and she stood by my side until it was all done.

I ended up taking a cab home. My family believed I tried to rob the man. My friend only wanted to know if the man had raped me. I was traumatized, but God kept me. I stopped that methadone program that same day and I have never been to one since. I put down that needle and only used drugs when I had my own money. I stopped stealing and I left people alone. No one really cared about me, not even the cops. One day they received a complaint from one of the catholic grade schools, the same one my sisters had put my oldest daughter in. There was a man giving candy to the little girls at this school and he fit the same description that I had given the cops two months before about this guy who cut me. He was spotted by the teachers, so now they wanted to look closer at my case to see if it was the same guy. I went to the police station only because it was about little kids. When I got there I picked out the teachers' sketch of the man and they had picked out mine. It was the same man. Now, the hard part was asking me to stand on that school corner the next day to see if I could get him to come after me. The cops just wanted me to walk the street where he could see me and see if he would come after me. I told them they were crazy, but they told me it was for the sake of the children, not them. Reluctantly, I agreed to do it so that the children at that school would be safe. After all, where was my life going? Nowhere. This was the least I could do.

I met them the next day and I was scared. I had a few friends with me but they had to stay out of sight. I walked up and down the street about three times when all of a sudden he showed up. When he saw me he took off and I got his plate number again. This time we realized that one of the numbers I gave them was in the wrong place, but they knew this. They put a trace on the car this time and set him up at his house with his wife on the phone. He came running out of the house to hide his car, I guess, and they caught him. Traces of my blood were found in his car and on his boots. He was sent back to the institution where he had come from three months earlier. I seemed to always do good deeds for others, even in that dog eat dog world. I had a heart for others. There was nothing I wouldn't do for you if I could, but don't try to hurt me or use me. Then you had a serious problem out of me.

I decided, as I shared earlier, to settle down and stay off the streets. I was not ready to die and, man, it was getting crazy out there. Drugs were getting scarce and it seemed everything was going up in price. You weren't getting much for your money. When I started using and selling drugs, heroin was only three dollars for a street bag. Now it was up to twenty dollars and you did not even get half of what you got for three dollars. When you did get it, sometimes it wasn't good. It was garbage. There was really no need in me getting killed over trash, so I cut out street hustling, period. I started staying home more and just drinking.

At least I was safe there. I would purchase cocaine only when I had extra cash or I sold my TV or something stupid like that. My baby's father believed me when I told him I went to the store and when I came back the window was broke and the TV gone. The detective told him it was an inside job, but he believed me. Besides, a man from Chicago was not really going to believe the cops any way. I then realized that coke would have me running all night and I could not let him find out about that, so I slowed down for a while. That's when I got pregnant with my third child, a girl, as I discussed earlier.

When my daughter was born she was very dark and beautiful. I had to care for her because her father would not dare let my mother keep his child and drive her crazy like she did me. He said this even before she was born, so now I really had to change my life. I tried to do it, but staying home every day, all day, was hard. Changing diaper after diaper. Nothing else but sex and diapers. Boy, I felt like a rag that you use, wash and put up, use, wash and put up. No company was allowed in the house, so I would bring her down to the lobby every day and we would talk to who ever came in the lobby just to have company. Then one day I met a lady who used to work with my baby's father and she said she didn't know how you got stuck with him but that he had me locked down like a prisoner. She sounded like she understood what I was going through, and she agreed to keep my baby once in a while so I could go out. She keeps her daughter's baby so she could go out, so why not?

We all lived in the same building, so it worked out fine until one day he saw her in the hall and they got to talking. He told her he kept me on lockdown to keep me off the streets and from doing drugs. However, I was drinking like a fish and sleeping it off, and he did not know this until she told him. Boy, he snuck up on me one night after coming home from work and this big man slapped me so hard my head felt like it rang the door bell. I thought he had broken something, but he didn't. The lesson I learned from that was to be cool around the neighbors.

I started doing my coke and drinking but, again, only when I had the money. My sister would come over and babysit, but he told her not to come back anymore. He said she was not helping me by doing what she was doing. My sister told him that I needed to get out more. She said, "She lives like she is in jail and this is what's making her drink."

He got mad with her and started yelling like he was crazy. My sister left but not before she told me, "Girl, this is not about the baby; it is about him. He don't want anybody around you." He slammed the door and I looked at him with my one sober eye. That's when I began to see that this man was obsessed with me, a young girl that he wanted all to himself. I had one sober eye at all times so that I could keep a watch on my baby as I drank until she would fall to sleep.

I tried my best to be a good mother no matter how drunk or high I got. It was very tough because I did love my children. But I was stuck in two very different worlds. I started going out, not caring about what he said. I would cook and leave the house. Everybody made sure I got home safe before three o'clock in the afternoon because he was now back with his wife but he came to me everyday before he went to work and after work. One day I fixed his wagon. I called his wife's job and pretended that I was their insurance company calling about medical payments for their new baby. I said I needed to confirm her date of birth. I did not mean to hurt this women, but it was what it was. He came to my house that night and he was mad. I told him that if they needed the information then they were only doing their job. "Lets face it," I said, "you do have a baby girl now and if you were having a hard time telling your wife then now you don't have to; they did it for you. Look, you said because you have sons you needed to let these boys know about their sister so they will not end up with one another years later. So now you have that chance. As far as your wife is concerned, you two were not together when I got pregnant and it just happened. She has no choice but to accept her part in throwing you out to the wolves."

You see, I was always smart. I learned how to handle men at a very young age, so don't try to play me; you will get played. He never knew I did this, but I did apologize to his wife later on once I got saved. I wrote her and asked her to forgive me for any hurt I had caused her through the years, but it was not all my fault. I found out once that she took my daughter with her to visit her family in the south. I did not know this at the time. My daughter's father led me to believe that he was taking her to meet his family in Chicago, but he lied. She took my baby with her down south, but there was no harm done to her that I know of. This women still loves my daughter and she told me not to get involved in their affairs. She is grown now and can decide for herself. My daughter has three brothers that she talks to and loves very much. I did not get involved again.

Eventually, my baby's father told me he had enough and was going to move back with his wife and kids for good, but would still provide for me and my daughter. He did this for a while. He also kept stopping by when he felt like it so I could not have any company. I guess he wanted to see how much control he really had over my life.

You see, some people will help you to stay sick even though they try to make it look like it is your fault. My mother believed she should have killed me at birth. I believe she tried to abort me, but I was born early instead. My mother said I did not want anything out of life. I was just like my no good daddy and would never amount to anything and she did not care if she never laid eyes on me again. I know from my heart and I need to share this now with everyone. My mother never meant a word she ever said about me. She was just so hurt and afraid to feel any more pain. She loved me but just could not show it or express it. My mother did not know how to love her children. Her mother died when she was only three years old. She had no one to teach her so she did the best she knew how to do. I'm not defending her wrong, just her lack of knowledge. I suffered much and so did my siblings because of this lack but their story is their own. I love my mother very much. You see, God shared these things with me as I matured in him.

My mother thought that this man would do good by me, but one day she saw who he really was. He told me to stop letting the baby ride her bike in the house. But it kept raining for days and I could not take her out, so I let her ride in the house. I did not realize that she had pulled the carpet up off the floor in a spot other than the one that was already pulled up. I heard him come in and I took the bike from her. We acted like we were watching TV. He started playing with her and I was fixing him something to eat. The hammer was on the kitchen counter, and when he came in the kitchen he saw it and asked what was I fixing. I told him I had been cleaning and left it out. He then went in the living room and looked around. He came back, grabbed the hammer and hit me in the head, knocking a hole in my head. I have that scar to this day. He saw the blood, got scared, grabbed my baby and ran out the house. I got myself together and went to the hospital. After they stitched me up, I went to the after hours club and got drunk. I had some coke but was told by my boy not to do it that night. He wanted me to wait until morning because he wanted me to test it and maybe sell it for him. He said he would give me a good deal on my selling it. I did as I said I would do, but it was hard to sleep that night with my head stitched up, my brain drunk and my emotions wanting that coke.

I did that coke early that morning. My baby was still somewhere with her dad. I think his wife had kept her for him. I don't really remember that part. Anyway, that coke was a money maker. I ran to him and he gave me some for my own use. I went to do it but my baby's father was coming in the door, so I hid it in the bathroom. He talked to me until he felt that he had me back on straight street. I just wanted him to leave or go to sleep so I could do my coke. I shot that coke as soon as he went to sleep, but I did not know I had overdosed. Thank God my baby ran in the room crying to her dad, screaming that I would not get up off the floor. He ran in there and found me on the floor with the needle still stuck in my neck. He kept putting cold towels on me and had the fan going. When I finally came around, he called me everything he could think of and left with the baby. He told me if I was not out of this apartment in two weeks he would have them throw me out. He said, "you sick b_____. I have done all I can do for you and I refuse to let you kill your dumb a___ around my child."

I felt like a load of concrete had been lifted off of me. You see, he was slicker than any man I had been with in the past. It always seemed like I was the one doing everybody else wrong, but they all wanted me to make them feel like they were all that and a cup off tea in the eyes of the world. I was sick in my own way, but they only pretended to see it and never really tried to understand me. My world was sick so I did not need some emotionally sick grown man holding on to their sick life through me.

I loved my child and I tried to get her back. I went to jail twice while I was trying to get her back. Once was for stealing. I got drunk and went out to see if I could steal enough merchandise to cop some coke. I decided not to trust myself to sell anymore drugs, especially coke. It would have killed me if I did not killed myself first. Then, I got arrested trying to steal when I got out. I said no more stealing. I had lost my touch. I went to detox, which was like my second home. They were glad to see me, as always, but I did not stay very long. My mind was on my baby. I asked to see her, but he only hung up the phone on me. Then, he would tell the guards to say he took the day off. Well, I started to feel that void in my heart again. Again, I started drinking and drugging really heavy. I saw my niece's mom one night and she started to cry. She loved me so very much and I loved her. She asked me what I was doing out there. Then she said, "Look at you. You have just thrown your life to the dogs. What do you want from these streets? What can they give you? Now you have nothing and no one that cares about you but me. These streets are going to be the death of you." I let her finish and gave her a hug and said, "I love you. Don't worry about me. I'm fine," and I walked away, still feeling her wet cheeks against mine.

I could not cry if I wanted to. It just was not in me to do so. I hung around with men at this time and a few women, but mainly men. Their wives knew me and I knew them. Respect was always there for them and their family. They were old enough to be my father or grandfather, so sex was not an issue. I could drink and not worry about what was going to happen next. One day I realized that this guy was doing more for me than any of the other women in the group, so I asked one of my older friends if this was true what I was seeing. She said, "I thought you and he had a thing going on. Let him tell it, he is at your house every night. I myself have carried him up there and watched him go in the building. I said, "He never came to my door. Are you serious?" He said, "On a stack of bibles. I would not lie to you, child. I took him myself." I began to put two and two together and, man, I got mad. He could have raped me or done all kinds of crazy things to me and everybody would have thought that I was going with this idiot. I told myself I would wait and play this thing out. I needed money so I was going to make this work for me. When he got paid I would ask him for money right in front of the other guys and he would give it to me. Then, one day I told him about his game and the lies he had been telling only because I was taking money from his sick wife. She was very ill with kidney trouble, I think, and I felt bad, so I came clean only because he had a very sick wife at home and I was taking money from her.

It was hard on the streets for me because I had a caring heart. There were certain things I could not do only because it would hurt someone else. I have seen many people shot to death right in front of me only because they could not let their pride go for the life of someone else.

Some people chose to die for dumb stupid reason. Me, I wanted to live to know me. I watched many young drug dealers and pushers gun each other down like they were robots instead of humans. I spent two years in the eighties going to so many funerals that I became numb to people that lost their loved ones. I overdosed at least four times, I think, and each time was more serious than the one before. I am sure that life left my body but not for a long period of time. God did not give death permission to hold me captive. I cannot say I've seen heaven or anything like that, but I did leave here and return.

Anyway, the same jerk that liked me and wanted everybody to think that he had been with me left a bunch of flowers and a big chocolate bunny at my front door on Easter. My baby's father came by to visit me but got upset when he saw the gifts outside the door. I did not know they were there. He came in with them in his hands, so I thought he was being nice and trying to make up with me. Then he asked me who was my new man. I looked at him and said, "What are you talking about?" He told me about the bunny and the flowers. He didn't believe me when I said I did not know where they had come from. He got jealous and threw them at me and told me he wanted me out of his apartment by the end of the week. I tried to explain, but he walked out.

I went to sleep before the big drinking party I had planned for the holiday weekend. When I woke up, I took my bath and I got dressed. As I was getting ready to leave I picked up this razor and put it in my sneakers before I left the house, not even knowing why I had done that. I went out and had a great time. It was about day break when I got home and went to sleep. When I got up it was Easter morning and I started on my way to drink some more. About two hours into my drinking I ran into the guy that had left the gifts at my door and we had a drink together. All of a sudden he ask me if I liked his gift. When he said this I reached down, took out the razor and started cutting on him. I had snapped just that quick. He started running and I was running right behind him. The cops had a mobile station on the main strip so he was running toward it when I sliced him across his back again. I turned and hid behind the people that I was hanging with and they took the razor and cleaned off my hands just as four cop cars came around the corner looking for me. I went over to them and they arrested me. I went to jail for women in Niantic, Connecticut until my court date. This man would not quit, however. He sent me money orders every week while I was locked up and also tried to come to see me. This man had lost his mind. On the day of my court appearance he came to court to drop all charges against me. They had to let me go with probation because they never found a weapon.

By then I was tired of the streets and that kind of life. I was getting sicker everyday about needing a drink and wanting cocaine, but it seemed like I had no way out. Two weeks had passed and I ended up back in detox. This time it seemed a little different for me because they asked me about moving to a half-way house in Hartford, Connecticut to try to start over again with a clean slate. I had been in and out of Bridgeport Mental Heath Center so many times that they needed to try something else with me. They really cared about me, I could tell, because nobody else had ever come up with any plan of action for a change for me. Just dry her out and let her go. She will be back, they thought. I spoke to my niece's mom and she said it may do me some good to go there and stay and do what I was told to do. My baby's father said I would not stay, so why go up there bothering those people. But he said he would help me out if I was really serious about going.

I got scared and did not go back to the meeting that had been set up. I had my daughter and nobody wanted to keep her, so I couldn't really go. I felt stuck, but only for a moment. I had gotten my baby back after I came out of jail. My daughter's father thought this would keep me out of the streets, but it didn't. So now I had to find someone to leave her with until I got out of the program. I went to my niece's mother's house to ask her to keep my baby for me but she would not open the door. I knew she was home so I knocked real hard and left my daughter standing in the hallway. I yelled, "I will call you when I get to Hartford." I had no one else left to help me so the next morning I went to the hospital to see if I still had a chance to go to the half-way house I told them about not having anyone to leave my daughter with for ten months. Everybody wanted me to go but nobody seemed to want to really commit to helping me by keeping a four-year old little girl. I was told that I could leave that Friday, but if I did not show up not to bother about looking for that kind of chance from them again. I called my baby's father and told him where our daughter was. He made arrangements to pay her child support money every week and to keep her on the weekend. This really made things much easier for me. I then went to Hartford to start my life over. I enjoyed the half-way house set up. I could work the work area as long as I wanted inside and not be bothered by anyone. This was a work program and not much treatment was being done. I met a guy there who was from Bridgeport, as well, and he had come there four months ahead of me, so he looked out for me and we ended up hooking up. After being there ten months I left with him, moved into a rooming house and the drinking and drugging started all over again. At first it was every other weekend. Then it was every weekend and, finally, every day. My baby's father had been supporting me financially while I was in the program, but after I left with this guy he stopped sending the money. It was best because now I had him out of my life. He still loved me but I needed to move on even if he did not want to. I needed to live for me.

You see, people can and do want to control you and own you when they are putting out their hard-earned money on you. He made me feel guilty all the time because he was providing for me. It's not like I couldn't make money, but if someone is willing to pay your way, why not take it? I was tired of him, but I did love him because he was always there for me when no one else was. He protected me in one sense but, on the other hand, he was blindly helping me to stay addicted to a lifestyle that he had helped me create for myself. I wanted out of this life. I just did not know how it was going to happen. I did not want to die an addict.

I stayed with this new guy, but he had no heart. I didn't even see him as a man. He was a punk with no heart. He believed in roots and had crazy family superstitions. Every time I did something for him he thought about something dumb, like you're not supposed to buy a man a watch because he will watch his time staying with you. One day we went home for the weekend and when we got back we saw that someone had broken into our room. It was a small efficiency apartment. They had stolen most of my things, so I knew they were addicts. They also took my children's papers and my ID's, so I had to call the police and make a report because of my babies' papers. The next weekend I had a money order for our rent. I had not yet made it out, but I had put it up. This got stolen as well. Even though I was drunk, I put two and two together. This punk was bragging and telling people when we did things, not knowing they were coming back and stealing. But he was the one who stole the rent money order. He thought I was passed out on the bed, which I was, but I wasn't drunk. I never got to the point where I did not know what I was doing. I kept one eye open, as they say, and I saw him ease in the room and take the money order. I played like I did not see him and asked, "What are you doing? Getting ready for bed?" He said, "No, baby. I just came in to check in on my baby." I told him I was staying in for the rest of the night, and he said he was going to sit on the front porch for a little while longer with the guys from upstairs.

I did not know at that time that he had really taken the money order until the landlord came that morning and I went to look for it and it was not there. I remember seeing him at the table the night before, so I called his job to ask if he had moved the money order and he told me no. The money order had been on the table under a lamp and I told him I saw him at the table with the lamp in his hands. He told me he didn't touch the lamp or go near that table. I knew for sure then that he had his own interest at heart and that I now needed to take care of me. The landlord knew something went wrong and I shared with him what had happened. However, he did not want to hear what I had to say even though I was telling the truth. He knew I always paid my rent on time, drugs or no drugs, but he didn't want to hear it. I had no plans on being homeless ever again. I asked him if he would just give me time to get the money together. After the landlord had left I realized then that man would rob me blind if I did not get my head on right.

I stopped drinking so much. I would just sip or sit around listening to people lies as well as tell my own. I had a love for people and a fear of being alone, as well. I began to see from my own life and from listening to other people's sad stories that this was not the life I wanted to live. But I had no idea how to get out of it because I had tried and failed so many times. The devil had me believing that this was the life I was suppose to live. But, the devil is a liar.

I began to watch people. Even though I did drink and drug every weekend, I didn't seem to fit in. I was just there with them in the flesh. In my mind, somehow, I had moved away from them. I did not share any of these thoughts with anyone, but I continued to talk to the Lord about my failing life and my faults, not realizing that he was now manifesting this life-changing experience in me. Women would come to me after being beaten up by their men. Young school girls would talk to me even though I smelled of alcohol, telling me about their pain. I would pray for the Lord to help them because I knew I couldn't do it even though I wished I could. I couldn't even help myself. I didn't even realize that what I was doing was praying because I had no proper teaching or training about God. All I knew was he lived in a place called heaven. God is awesome. He was setting me up. Even as I tentatively listened to others through my drunk haze, he was establishing my ministry as well as bringing about my healing.

I was about to be evicted along with everyone else in the building because the police were shutting down the place due to unpaid taxes or something. It was a very clean, well-kept building. The tenants looked out for each other, but you didn't touch anyone's "get high." One day, a neighbor upstairs came down to my room. She had a check from her old man's job. At that time he was in jail for beating her up. Man, she weighed every bit of sixty-five pounds soaking wet. She wanted me to go with her to try and cash this check. I told her no, closed my door and locked it. What is wrong with people coming up here with stupid stuff, I thought. I had not had a drink yet because if I had I may have gone with her. That was the best thing I could have done that whole year other than to decide not to get wiped out drunk anymore.

I went upstairs to my drinking buddy's room and we got to talking and drinking and I had told her about it. She kept a problem with her man all the time. She was going out with an old married man and I could not understand it. Why fall in love with an old ugly man? Why not an old cute man? Then maybe I could understand a little bit about the mad love. But, please. I liked this lady as a neighbor very much, but she was drinking herself right into the grave. I kept trying to help her even though I was not at my best. I did not want to see her go down the way she was. One night I heard her knocking at my door and when I opened the door her lips were a blue-black color. I called the ambulance and they took her to the hospital. Her kidneys had failed. I felt bad for her. Her family lived in Georgia and I could not get in touch with them. Eventually, she came out alive but she needed nursing care and had to stop the drinking. She thought she had found a way to get around that. She tried to sneak and drink.

I left her alone as far as being a drinking partner, but we cooked and ate and talked a lot. She still tried to hold on to that ugly, fat married man who now had control of her money and handled all her affairs. I did not like him but he was not mine to be concerned about. I want to tell women all over the world if you do not want God's curse on you, please leave these no good married men alone. They don't mean you any good and God is not going to bless any mess you've tried to put together. It's just not going to happen. You are digging your own emotional grave. It gets harder and harder to feel real love or even desire it.

Now, I was out there all by myself even though that man, that punk, still lived with me. I let him think whatever he wanted to think. I just could not understand how a dude can say he is a man and has no throw down in any area of his life. This was the first and believe me when I say this because I prophesy this to myself: In the Name of Jesus, I will never have another man in my life that has short comings in every area of his life. Ladies, a man that cannot fix one error in his life with another area has a sure problem with me because I cannot make something what it ain't. And, brother, if you are short on every end, please keep stepping. There is no need in you coming around me to make me have to repent to the Father who already knew from the beginning that you, homes, are short. I'm just being real and telling you what I'm not going to go for. Many of us women go after these married men and want to just take over that man's life. He is not yours to do that in the first place. You forget that he belongs to someone else already. I hear a lot of women say that they're going to take him from his wife and they believe this nonsense. You never have a married man to yourself, and just like he cheated on his wife with you, sooner or later he is going to cheat on you. Now you've got soul ties and may be picking up evil spirits from him that he picked up from the women he's slept with.

Anyway, I started staying in the house more. My life began to slow down just a little, but I could feel my own thoughts again and I wanted out more than ever. Everyone around me was either dying or going to jail. I just felt so very tired and wanted out. But how? I had done all I could do out there in the world. What was left for me to do? I wished I could just fall asleep for good. I did not want that for real, but I had begun to realize how much I had done and been through and it overwhelmed me. I spent twenty-two years' worth of energy running but going nowhere and doing nothing. I had not accomplished anything I ever wanted to do nor did I know what I wanted to do or could do. I had lost sight of life. It seemed that my life had been swallowed up in a dark cocoon.

One Wednesday morning my friend suggested that we just lay around the house. He said he was going to call out from work, which was his choice. He mentioned that we had not really done anything together in awhile. He and I both loved to dress up and just go walking. Everyone said we looked good together. He had a beautiful voice and he would sing to me. He had a great smile and I had a crazy laugh. We had some fun. It was not always hell, but my days of fun were numbered, believe me. Anyway, we went to the package store and the grocery store, and we came home, cooked breakfast, had our few drinks and watched some TV. Then he suggested we go for a walk. We both put on our jogging suits and left the apartment.

We ended up on Albany Avenue at a friend's house who liked me as a sister. He looked out for me and just liked to hear me talk, I guess. My former drinking buddy who had asked me to help her cash her man's check was there and so was he. They were having a little get together because he had come home from jail. Now I saw why he wanted to take this day off from work. It had nothing at all to do with me but his running partner, who was home from jail. I just went along. I did not care anyway. We kept drinking and because I had cut down on my drinking I started to get drunk really fast. I asked to go home. I could feel myself getting too high too fast, so I finally just started to walk by myself.

I stayed at the house and slept for about two hours and I woke up realizing that he never followed me home. I got dressed to go back over to where I had left him on Albany Avenue. I got in the hallway and my mind told me to go back and get my razor. I had not carried that thing in a long time, but I went back in the room and finally remembered what I had done with it. I put it in my sneaker on the side then I left. I looked back at the street and the houses as I was going through the shortcut pathway, not knowing why but just looking back. Thoughts of the old couple on the first floor crossed my mind. They looked after me as if I was their daughter, but we just drank together every single day. That old man made sure that when he and his wife had a wake up drink, I had one too.

I said to myself as I walked, not understanding anything, "They can take care of themselves. They've been doing it all these years." I finally arrived back at the friend's house on Albany Avenue. When I got there I was told that my friend had gone to the store to re-up on their alcohol. I asked how long he had been gone and the guy said, "He should be on his way back. Sit in here with me." So I went in his back room where they were smoking weed. I was not big on smoking weed. It only made me eat and laugh and I seemed to do one of those quite well on my own. But I smoked a little. Then my man came in. We all had a few drinks and I went to get some of the chicken he told me to get that was on the kitchen table. Man, all hell broke loose. This dude started cursing at me and demanding that I give him his money for the check I had stolen from of his mail box, which I had already told him I did not do. The friend of mine whose house we were at, along with my boyfriend, came into the kitchen to see what was going on. As I told them both what was happening the guy whose apartment it was said, "Man, I'm not going to have this in my house. If this women said she did not break in your mail box you're just going to have to believe her or take this noise somewhere else."

I just felt I needed to leave, so I said to my boyfriend, "Man, let's go. I need to get up out of here." He said, "Ok, baby. Let me finish up this last drink I had before you two started this mess." I stood by the bedroom door for about five minutes, then I turned and started to leave the apartment when the dude who had cursed me jumped in front of me. I said, "Man, please do not start with me. I'm not the one for you to keep bothering, ok? Really, I'm not." I tried to go around him again with a polite "excuse me, please", but he wanted to end his life that day, I could tell. I stood there and I said again, "Please move out of my way." This man raised his hand and sucker punched me in my lip. I have the mark to this day. My mouth started to bleed. My brain shut down and, my God, I lost all control. If I ever had any, it was gone. I pulled out my razor from my sneakers and sisters, I tell you no lie, I went to work on home boy. I cut him and he began to run. You see, a razor cut stings so you really don't know you are cut until you feel the stinging sensation.

He began to run out the front door that he should have so kindly let me out of in the first place. Now he was more than glad to open that door. He kept calling me a b_____ and running at the same time. Even though I was drunk now and my blood pressure was up I stayed on his butt. My friend came running downstairs yelling for me to stop. He pulled me from behind to prevent me from cutting this dude for about the fourth or fifth time. He grabbed me, took me upstairs clean my hands off and gave my boyfriend the razor. He told him to put it in the street drain so it would never be found for sure. He looked at me and said, "I'm so glad I like you and you like me, my sister, because you just did some real damage to that dude. Man, they are going to try and throw the key away on you, but as long as they don't find that razor you have a fighting chance. You cut that man in his face, the back and who knows where else." I said that I had told him to leave me alone, but he just had to punch me. He said, "I don't think you have to worry about home boy punching another women as long as he lives. He will survive, but you know jail time awaits you." Then he hugged me.

My boyfriend came back upstairs all scared out of his punk mind. "Buttercup, why did you cut him," he asked. They called the police. "Buttercup, I love you. What do I do now?" Before his "Buttercup" could answer him the police stormed into my friend's house, guns drawn. I just cannot remember anything after I heard him say, "Officer, you don't need to come up in my crib like this. She is right here. He punched her in her mouth real hard over a check that he said she stole. He even told me himself that she did not break into his mailbox. We all had been drinking and this is the result of it all. They got into a fight and he got cut. We did not see what she cut him with or even if she did it. It happened in the hallway and a lot of guys were out there. She did not have a weapon on her when we pulled them apart." I left there feeling like my life had just ended for good. A peace from within came upon me but I had too much going on to examine it. I was locked up, charged with first degree assault and taken to women's prison in Niantic to await trial. As far as my boyfriend was concerned, my family saw him two weeks after I went to jail but he never told them I was locked up. Maybe he thought they knew but I never saw him again.

Well my story must stop here but only for a moment. To see the transformative power of God pick up my next book "From Prison to Present". In the meantime be blessed.